M000237672

MAZAMA
THE PAST 100 YEARS

Life and Events in the Upper
Methow Valley & Early Winters

COMPILED BY DOUG DEVIN

Seattle, Washington
Portland, Oregon
Denver, Colorado
Vancouver, B.C.

Dedication

To all the men and women, past and present, who
have given Mazama its character of today and
its direction for tomorrow.

Proceeds from the sale of this book will be donated
to
The Okanogan County Historical Society,
Shafer Museum & Mazama Community Club

MAZAMA
The Past 100 Years

Cover Photographs:

1. The Angus McLeod Building in Mazama served as a hotel, saloon, store, post office, and community gathering place for many years. The only identification found with this picture was "Dad Callahan 3rd." This could have been Lester Holloway's and Bill Looney's father-in-law.

2. Early skiers at Early Winters in the late 1920s, back to front: Earl Short, Bud Short, Wayne Grant, and Shirley Grant. The Grants lived on H.E.S. 93 and the Shorts lived on H.E.S. 92. This photograph was taken on H.E.S. 92.

Copyright © 1997 Douglas W. Devin
All rights reserved. No part of this publication may be
reproduced without express written permission of the publisher, except in the case of brief
quotations embodied in critical articles or reviews.

ISBN # 0-89716-701-5
LOC 96-071310
01.0047
Cover design: David Marty
Editing: Anne Melley
Production: Elizabeth Lake

First printing April 1997
10 9 8 7 6 5 4 3 2 1

Peanut Butter Publishing
Pier 55, Suite 301 1101 Alaskan Way • Seattle, WA 98101-2982
(206) 748-0345 • FAX (206) 748-0343
Portland, OR (503) 222-5527 • Denver, CO (303) 322-0065
Vancouver, B.C. (604) 688-0320 • Scottsdale, AZ (602) 947-3575
e mail: pnutpub@aol.com
WWW home page: http://www.pbpublishing.com

Printed in Canada

ACKNOWLEDGMENTS

Many sources have been consulted in compiling the information in this book. Below is a list of individuals, publications, museums, libraries, and other sources that contributed information. I offer my sincere thanks to all of these sources, without whom this book would not have been possible. My apologies for any omissions; they are entirely unintentional.

Individual Contributors

Ella Black
Harold Bowers
Bob Cram
Hank Dammann
Grace Devin
Stan Dick
Eleanor Drake
Barbara Duffy
Darrell Ford
Walt Foster
Barry George
Roy Goodall
Sandy Haase
John Hayes
Harold Heath
Hazel Holloway
Chuck Hotchkiss
Roy & Doris Kumm
Bill Laney
Della Northcott
Vernon Overturf
Larry Patterson
Don & Sally Portman
Joe Scaylea (photographs)
Don & Dorothy Shafer
Bud Short
Bill & Martha Stewart

Wally Stewart
Bill Wehmeyer
Mabel Wehmeyer
Gordon Welch
Elsie Wilson

Books and Newspapers

Zora Ballard's Diary
Ethel Holloway's Diary
John McKinney's Diary
Late Frontier, by Bruce Wilson
Methow Valley Pioneers, by Dale Dibble
Northwest Discovery, vol. 4, June, 1983
Methow Valley News
Methow Valley Journal
Okanogan County Heritage
Seattle Weekly
The Seattle Times

Libraries, Museums, and Other Sources

Okanogan County Historical Society
Shafer Museum
Transamerica Title Company
University of Washington Library
Washington State Historical Society,
  Tacoma (Photos on page 22 & 84)
U. S. Forest Service, Winthrop

Special thanks for guidance and direction for this book go to Sally Portman, author of *The Smiling Country*, a wonderful, scholarly history of the Methow Valley. And to my wife, Grace, for her invaluable assistance and encouragement.

Doug Devin

Table of Contents

Table of Contents

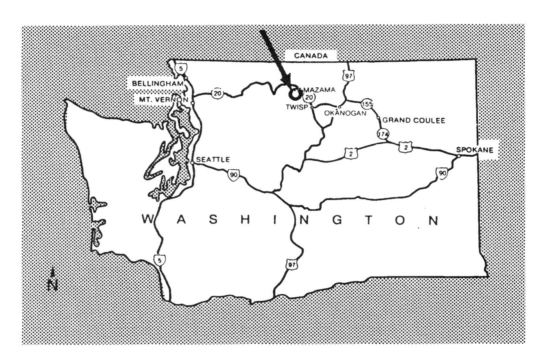

Mazama is located at the upper end of the Methow Valley that was the "end of the road" until the North Cascades Highway was completed in 1972. The remote location, climate and inaccessibility of the area led to a delayed development condition and life style that attracts many who today are looking for an alternative to the growing urban culture. Its remoteness still exists for about one third of the year when the North Cascades Highway is closed, but its notoriety is no longer a secret.

The Mazama area is nestled on the eastern edge of the Cascade Mountains. This 1970s photo, looking west shows the upper Methow Valley between Cedar Creek and Early Winters Creek on the right and Little Boulder Creek on the left. In the lower center of the picture, the road from Highway 20 can be seen crossing the river to Lost River Road and the commercial area containing Mazama's store, community center and the ranch house.

The large forested mountain in the center of the photo is Sandy Butte, the area proposed for a ski hill that created controversy for decades starting in 1970. The rugged snow covered peak behind Sandy Butte is Mt. Gardner.

Introduction

This book is an account of the development and growth of the area of the Upper Methow Valley known as Mazama. It includes excerpts from several persons' diaries and letters, and information and dates from other publications. Important sources of information for this book were old issues of the *Methow Valley Journal,* published from 1912 to about 1942, and the *Methow Valley News* which started publishing in 1902.

Other invaluable sources of information were numerous longtime residents of the area whose recollections were either handed down in writing or told to me personally. Even with the aid of these wonderful sources of information, I have, without question, omitted important incidents and failed to acknowledge individuals who played major roles in the development of the area. For this I must apologize up front. The omissions are accidental and due to ignorance on my part.

The area covered by this book encompasses the land west of Winthrop, Washington, and east of the Cascade Mountains. Words, maps, and photographs hardly begin to do justice to the beauty and majesty of the area. The mountains, valleys, rivers, and streams comprise a breathtakingly beautiful panorama that cannot be adequately described by words or pictures. However, words and pictures are all that are available to tell this story, so please feel free to use your imagination to enhance what I have described if you are not already familiar with this magnificent area.

The area known today as Mazama (pronounced like "Alabama" by old-time locals) was identified by various other names in early times. These other names are mentioned where appropriate in the book. Winthrop and the Slate Creek mining district have famous histories and are recorded in a number of other publications. In this book, these areas are mentioned only to the extent they affected the development of the Mazama area.

Researching the history of an area like this is a fascinating and never-ending endeavor. There is always one more person to interview and another lead to pursue. At some point, however, I found it necessary to stop gathering information and assemble and organize the material I had already collected. In the future, more research will undoubtedly uncover more information and update the information contained in this book.

The book is divided into two parts, preceded by a brief discussion of homesteading in general. Part I, entitled "On the Road to Mazama," begins in Winthrop and discusses points of interest one encounters along the road all the way to Lost River. The information in that section was provided by longtime residents Bill and Martha Stewart and Roy and Doris Kumm. Part II is a chronological account of the development of the area. It discusses particular individuals and families, how they came to settle where they did, and their activities in and contributions to the area. It also attempts to capture snapshots of life and activity during each decade from the time the first white men came in to the area until the mid-1990s.

Chapters in Part II, covering my perceptions of recent decades of history regarding Early Winters, contain many more details than other chapters in the book for several reasons. First, I was intimately familiar and involved with the activity involving Early Winters. Second, it was probably the most significant happening in recent times to affect the area and created issues and events which gave the area national attention. Finally, the Early Winters project, along with other similar events in the West, opened a new era in the history of the development of western lands, and set a precedent concerning the evolution of rural properties, communities, and economies for the years to come.

There are many persons better qualified to write the history of the Mazama area than I, particularly since I did not arrive in the area until 1959. In fact, I spent many years trying to persuade some of the early settlers to record their recollections, but I was unsuccessful in my efforts. Thus, I resorted to collecting some of their stories, either by note taking or tape recording. I had hoped this would generate some interest on the part of an experienced author in preserving the history of the area. This ploy didn't work either, and I have become author by default.

Doug Devin
Mazama, Washington

Homesteading - The Beginning of Development

The United States Congress passed an Act on May 20, 1862, "To Secure Homesteads to Actual Settlers on the Public Domain." Filings were made at the nearest land office, which, at that time, for Okanogan and the Methow was in Waterville. After the filings had been "established and duly consummated in conformity to law," the President of the United States granted to "said claimant, the tract of land described TO HAVE AND TO HOLD."

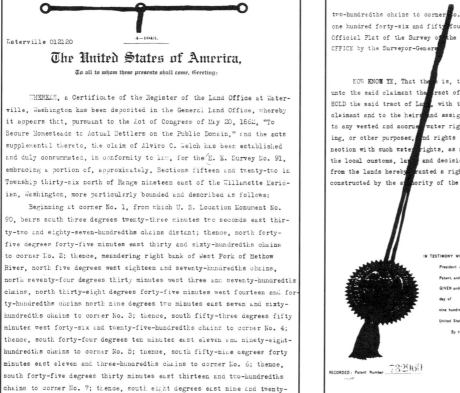
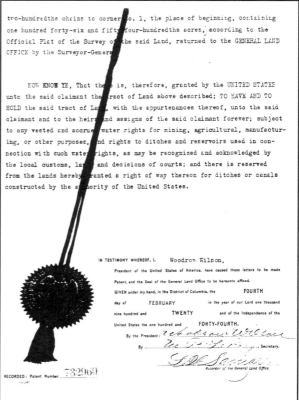

This patent for HES 91 was issued by President Woodrow Wilson on February 4, 1920. It is complete with the seal of the United States and the official accroutrement of a red ribbon attached.

Most of the land in the Methow Valley was obtained in this manner. By the time the Methow was changed from Indian land to eligible homestead land, most of the West had already been settled and the days of the great land rush had ended.

In the early 1900s, the United States Forest Service, or Forest Reserve, had been established and mountain and forest lands came under its management. An Act in 1906 provided for National Forest Homestead Entry Surveys (or HES) of agricultural lands within national forests. The Act was geared towards lands more suitable for agriculture than for forestry purposes. Most of the land in the Mazama area was unsurveyed and was part of the national forest at that time. Thus, all of the claims in the area were made in accordance with the 1906 HES Act. Many of the current descriptions of land in the area contain references to an HES number, and county tax parcels often carry the number as identification. Many of the parcels discussed in this book are also referred to by HES number.

Because most of the land was unsurveyed, many farmers and homesteaders filed claims based on descriptions and surveys they made themselves, using measurements based on witness trees, rocks, rivers, and streams. These old surveys were usually amazingly accurate, especially considering the instruments that were used, and the descriptions continued to be used when the land is sold or divided.

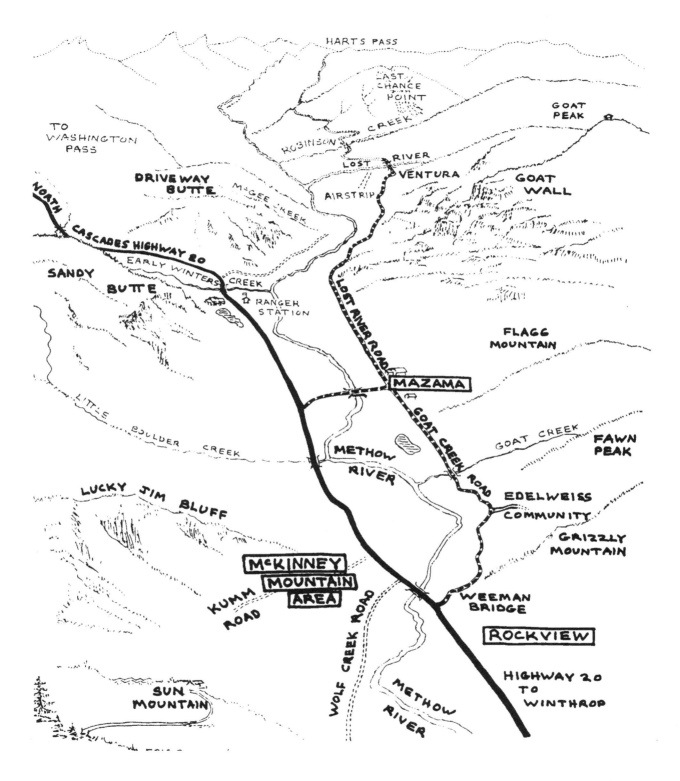

This illustration of the Mazama area, while not to scale, identifies the important areas of both early and current Mazama.
                                                                        Artist: Eric Burr

14

Part I - A Geographical Recollection

On The Road to Mazama
Prologue

In an effort to record some information about the people who settled the Mazama area, the author took a leisurely drive from Winthrop to Lost River on two occasions in 1990. On one occasion, the author was accompanied by Bill and Martha Stewart. Martha came to the Methow Valley in 1902 as a young girl. Her parents, Mr. and Mrs. Tom Sloane,

Roy and Doris Kumm in 1993.

Bill and Martha Stewart in 1992.

homesteaded on HES 200 and HES 202 in Mazama. The second trip through the area was with Roy and Doris Kumm. Roy was the son of Frank Kumm, an early settler in the McKinney Mountain area, and spent most of his life in the Mazama area.

On both trips, the author took notes and tape recorded the comments of the passengers as the trip progressed. The Stewarts and the Kumms passed on their knowledge of who lived in what house, who farmed what land, who sold what, who bought what, and a few amusing anecdotes. The Stewarts' and the Kumms' memories were quite sharp and there was little discrepancy among any of their stories. The trips brought back many memories and stories that had long been forgotten.

What follows are the Stewarts' and the Kumms' recollections and stories, often using their own words, that came to mind along the road to Mazama. The numbers appearing in parentheses represent locations on the map below.

Winthrop to Weeman Bridge

In the early days, as the road left Winthrop heading west, it wandered around the foot of the hills. About one mile out of town on the left, there was an early farm in the big field (1). The identity of the homesteader wasn't known, but an early owner of the farm was a party named Clark who had lived in the eastern United States. It is thought that Mr. Clark was a friend of Guy Waring who had purchased this land on Waring's speculation that construction of a railroad was imminent. The Edson family leased the property from Clark and put up lots of hay. The house and barn were near the present road.

The house by the river, which could still be seen in 1990, was leased by O.K. Gullion who farmed the upper portion of the field. The field was flood irrigated, and in the 1948 flood, the ditch washed out and the field eventually went to barnaby weeds. Don Dagnon returned it to production with the installation of a sprinkler system in the mid 1980s. In 1993, as the result of a marriage breakup, a developer subdivided the farm into large tracts.

On the bench above, on the right, another Clark, Gale Clark, had a house (2) and farmed dry land. A fellow by the name of Levi Hicks, who Bill Stewart claimed spent most of his time making moonshine, lived down by the river near here. The old road ran over the hill, unlike the present road which runs by the river. The old road ran past the Goudy place (3) which currently is the east end of the Heath Ranch. The Goudy house and barn sat up on the hill near an apple tree. It is located by following the road which in the 1990s leads to a highway department gravel pit.

Across the river was one of the oldest homesteads, the Thompson place (4). Fred Thompson came to the area in 1888, before his brother, George, arrived, and took up that land because it was free of trees. As it turned out, the absence of trees was because the claim sat on a pile of rocks. Kikendall had a house (5) on the river next to Thompson, but most of his property was on the hill across the river next to Goudy.

Indians had built a number of pit houses (6) on the Kikendall property on both sides of the river. The holes still exist and several have been excavated by historians. There are numerous stories about how this area was active in Indian times. The stories are substantiated by the number of pit house sites, Indian relics, and arrowheads found nearby. Some theorize that an Indian battle was fought on the plain where Wolf Creek flows into the

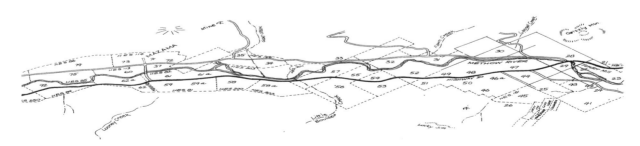

Methow. Legend has it that after the battle, Indians would not cross the area after dark.

The Three Mile Bridge was the major crossing point of the Methow River for years. The bridge was located just above the point at which Wolf Creek flows into the Methow River.

Across the road from what was the Heath home in the 1990s, near the pond, was the place owned by S. Virginia Moore. At the time S. Virginia owned the land, the pond was known as Moore's Slew (7).

Before her marriage to John Moore, S. Virginia Moore was Sally Shipp, an artist who grew up as a Chicago society girl. John was interested in the Slate Creek mines and brought his new wife to the Rockview ranch in 1902. Their daughter, Betty, was born three months before John was killed in a snow slide near the Chancellor Mine. S. Virginia had to run the ranch to make a living for herself and her daughter. When Betty was old enough for school, S. Virginia rented the ranch and moved to Twisp. She ran the Methow Valley Inn for many years. Her daughter, Betty, married Frank Holec and moved back to the ranch in the 1930s. Later, in the 1940s, George Cooper built a little sawmill by the pond on the ranch.

West of the Moore place, in the area where the Big Valley Ranch shops are located, was the Albert Ventzki homestead (8). A bachelor,

The Goudy Ranch is in the foreground and the Vensky Ranch is beyond. Travel up the "Goudy Grade," seen here, was the route up the valley until the new highway was built in the early 1990s and eliminated the hill with a very large road cut. (3)

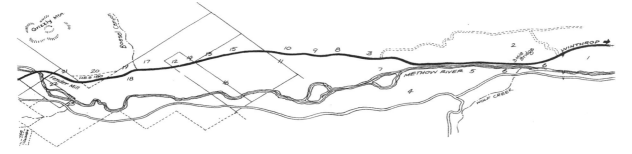

Albert and Emil Ventzke at Albert's homestead before it burned. It was located below the area where the Big Valley shops are sited in the 1990s. There were three Ventzkes who were active in the valley. In addition to Albert, there was Emil,who had a homestead up the Chewuck, and Charles, who was an engineer with an office and home in Winthrop. (8)

Albert built a log house and cleared most of the fields in that area. Today, the fields are farmed by Big Valley. The log house burned down and Albert moved into a little 14-foot shack on the other side of the road.

Around the curve beyond the shops, there is a little bench on the right (north) side, just above the road. This was the site of the Rockview Hall (9), a popular early-day gathering spot, built as a Grange hall and dance hall. Active in the 1920s and 1930s, it is said to have held more dances than any other place in the valley. Over time, the hall fell into disrepair and was eventually torn down in the 1950s.

About five miles from town, across from the Big Valley corrals, stands a house built by Wayne Carrell. Next to that is a house (10) built by the Holcomb family on a piece of land they bought from Wayne. The next

Eleanor Kent Drake and her young son, Gordon,in front of the 1950 remains of the old Rockview Hall. (9)

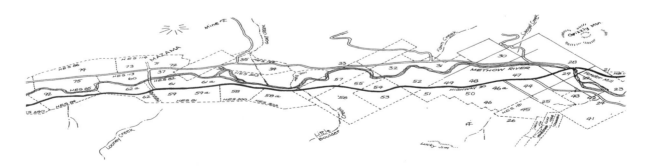

The shed on the left (11) which stood in this 1990 picture, went down in the 1995 winter snows. The house in the middle of the picture is the old Rockview school(12), which was moved to this location and now serves as a home.

The little house which sat on the property in the 1990s was moved in from a half mile up the valley. It had been the old Rockview school (12) which sat above the road near the Cooper place.

Situated on the next property down the road, just past mile marker 187, sits a white house with a screened porch (15) (see page 74) and a big barn. Both were built by William Wehmeyer, who came to the valley in 1892. He also built a big barn. The house was restored

place down the road was built by Logan Graves. Logan's house burned down in the 1940s and only a shed (11) remained. In the winter of 1995, the shed collapsed. Roy Kumm said that the Cooper boys were living there before the fire and *"they would jump out of bed and go to town to eat breakfast and leave the electric blanket on, and that's what set the house afire."* This part of the valley got electric power in about 1940, but safety practices had not yet been learned.

H.H. (Hank) Johnson homestead, later known as the Cooper place, stood next to the Wehmeyer home until moved up the valley in the 1990s. At the turn of the century, there was a sawmill in the vicinity of the house, but later the Rockview Mill was on this ranch down by the river. Johnson was Wehmeyer's brother-in-law and Zora Ballard's father. (14)

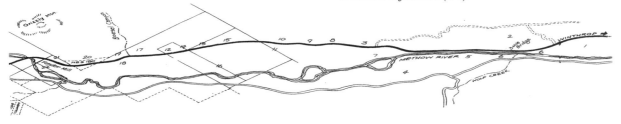

The Wehmeyer family gathers at the site where they will build their home at the turn of the century. Notice the rock outcrop at the top of the picture. (15)

Farther along, near the river, is the Rockview Mill (16). It was built by Hank Johnson and his son-in-law, Hazard Ballard. The mill operated for a number of years in the early 1900s.

The Boesel homestead (17) extended from the hillside to the river. Locals named Boesel Canyon and Boesel Creek, located on the homestead, after the family. Maps from the turn of the century show that a sawmill and a school were temporarily located here.

in 1996, but the barn was destroyed by snow in the winter of 1994.

The next house (13) was built by William's son, Charlie, and in 1990s was occupied by Walt Holcomb. Next to Charlie's house was the homestead house of H.H. (Hank) Johnson (14), William Wehmeyer's brother-in-law. The Johnson homestead was later bought by the Cooper family and is often called the "Cooper Place" even though Hank Johnson built and occupied it. The house was moved up the valley below Little Boulder Creek in about 1993.

The Charlie Wehmeyer homestead house occupied by the Walt Holcomb family in the 1990s. Notice the change in the vegetation over 100 years. (13) Notice rock outcrop in this picture and in the picture above.

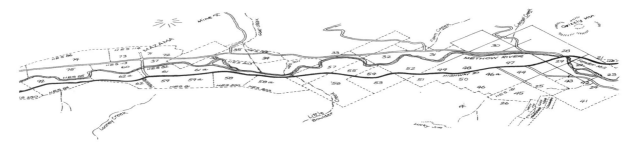

Carl Perry's house. (20)

Down the grade on the left was the house built by Rockview Mill worker Jessie Smith (18). The next place, owned by the Elders, extended on both sides of the road. The house burned down but the crab apple tree (19) is still growing. Carl Perry built the house and barn on the right (20), about seven miles from Winthrop, in the mid-1920s. The place was home-steaded by Fred Wehmeyer who mostly worked for the Forest Service, but Carl made most of the improvements to the property.

At this point in the journey on the road to Mazama, Grizzly Mountain is on the right. A few feet from the present road, east of mile marker 185, one can still see Indian paintings on the rocks (21). On the left is where the Fender Mill once stood (22). The old road turned left before the mill and went down to the river where there was a low water crossing known as the Perrine Ford (23). It came out just above Hancock Creek across the Methow River.

In 1990, the Fender Mill site was covered with cottonwood trees and brush. When the mill was operating, however, a big mill pond was located where the fish screen now sits. A few hundred feet south were the mill, a large burner, shops, and several little buildings to house some of the workers. The mill operated mainly during the summer, but all winter, teams of horses and men hauled logs. Bill Stewart said, *"at one time they had 26 outfits working."* Part of the mill burned at one point and was rebuilt. Ownership of the mill went from Fender to a Mr. Wetzel. When Wetzel went broke in 1937 and the mill fell into receivership, and Otto Wagner purchased it in 1939. Wagner eventually tore the mill down and moved it to Twisp.

The other side of the river was known as the McKinney Mountain area. The ford crossed near the Bert Perrine and the Morrow places (24). This area was homesteaded by a Mr. Hancock. Adjoining this were the sites on which John McKinney built his cabin (25) and Lester Holloway started his ranch (26). It was also the home of Roy and Doris Kumm (25).

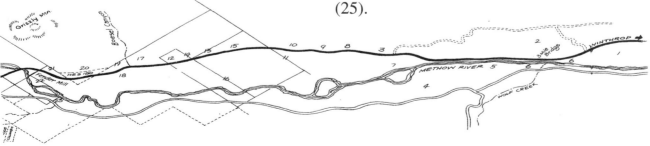

Fender Mill pond located just down river from the Weeman Bridge.(22)

Weeman Bridge to Mazama on the Goat Creek Road

The Weeman Bridge was named after the Weeman family who homesteaded the land up river from the Fender Mill on both sides of the river. The house and barns (28) were on the hill as you start up the Goat Creek Road where the Drakes lived from 1962 to 1985. The original house burned and was rebuilt by Don Drake. The original Weeman homestead extended down the hill and across the river, where the family grew a big field of red clover because it was too wet to grow alfalfa and other crops.

Over the years, several bridges were located at the site. The first bridge was built in 1911 or 1912 and was washed out by high water in 1932. The next bridge was washed out during the 1948 flood. The one-way steel bridge which replaced it stood until 1988 when the new highway was built and a concrete bridge was built (29).

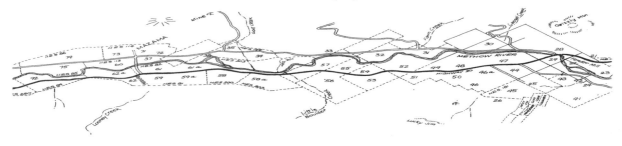

Farther up the Goat Creek Road was the Joshua Cassal ranch (30). Homesteader Burt Perrine sold it to Joshua when Burt took over his father-in-law's place, the Hancock place. The house and barn were on the bench above, just below the field. Joshua irrigated out of Fawn Creek and put up enough hay in both fields for 30 or 40 milk cows and two barns. The original road went up Fawn Creek, came back along the bench, and followed the river. The present alignment of the road was established in the early 1970s with the opening of Washington Pass and the rebuilding and surfacing of this county road. The Edelweiss development is now located on the site. Near where the Edelweiss utility building and campground area are situated, there once lived an Indian family, Ed and Lucy Walsh (31). Ed cut logs and worked in the mill.

Farther along the road, there is a log house and an old barn on land homesteaded by a bachelor named Jake Grazen (32). Guy Pitt later lived there, did a little farming, and cut logs and hauled them to the mill. Guy was remembered as spending considerable time drinking beer, *"about two gallons per day,"* Roy Kumm guessed. Guy was also famous for his "home brew" during prohibition days, and there are still a few old-timers who remember a visit to Guy's place. He would haul up bottles from his well, where the beer was kept cool, and all would sit under the willow tree enjoying the brew. Guy had the nickname of "Two-tone" because when he would get excited, his voice would crack. The present log cabin was built after Guy's house was gone.

The present road enters Forest Service land (33) at this point and continues past the Forest Service road that follows Goat Creek, then down a hill, through a gully, and on to the present bridge over Goat Creek. The creek formerly ran through the gully and was moved to its present location on the ridge during the flood of 1948.

Just past the new Goat Creek bridge is HES 199, Joshua Cassal's original homestead (34). Josh found the land and staked his claim in the winter, but when the snow melted he found that all he had was a pile of rocks. Nevertheless, he built a three-story boarding house on the north side of the road with thirteen or fourteen rooms (35). At that time, the Montana Mine was operating farther up Goat Creek, and Josh rented out rooms to the miners.

It is also believed that the first floor of Josh's boarding house contained the first Mazama post office in 1900, run by Minnie Tingley. Minnie married Jack

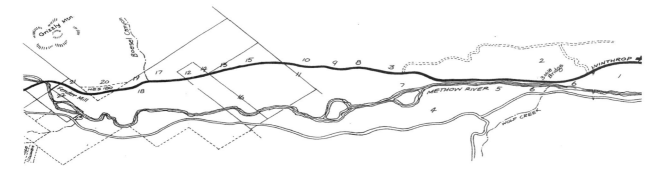

Stewart who owned the next place, HES 203. The person who homesteaded HES 203 is not known. Jack Stewart, a mining engineer from England, moved his mill from the lower Methow to the Flag Mine

Mazama Post Office location in the mid 1920s was in this building which was probably the McLeod Bldg. An old prospector, Alec McLean, holds young Bud Short for the camera.

in Mazama around 1900. Jack went on to mine in the Barron area, but returned to farm his Goat Creek ranch (36) when the mines played out.

The Stewarts built a very nice home and barn which became one of the show-places of the Mazama area. The barn burned long after the Stewarts left. The house stood for many years and in the 1970s it was remodeled as a guest ranch for summer and winter visitors. Unfortunately, the ranch burned the week before it was to have opened.

Just down the river from the present Mazama Community Club, HES 113 (37) was located on the left (south) side of the road. It was homesteaded by Angus McLeod who did a little farming but also built a hotel, bar, and boarding house for miners. After the post office moved from Jack Stewart's building near Goat Creek, it was located in the McLeod building from 1918 until 1928. McLeod also owned the land up river from the present Mazama Bridge and he allowed the community to have a picnic area and an outdoor dance floor near the river (60). The site was the scene of many gala Fourth of July festivals. Up river from the community building was a baseball field for the Mazama home team. By the 1990s, the area was overgrown by trees and no trace of the early day festivities was visible. Today the ball field is used as a roping area where hopeful rodeo riders gather to test their skills.

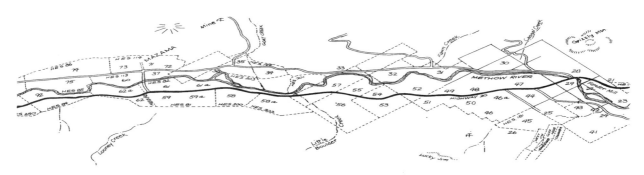

McKinney Mountain to Mazama on Highway 20

Remains of this homesteader cabin, probably built by Mar Perrine on the Morrow place, reveal that living conditions were primitive, but the view of Grizzly Mountain and the upper Methow were excellent and indicate the homesteaders' tasteful priorities in site selection. (41)

Our journey returns to the Weeman Bridge area. On the south side of the Methow across from the Fender Mill sat the community of McKinney Mountain. The area is now served by the Wolf Creek Road and the Kumm Road. At the east end of the fields on the Wolf Creek Road are

the remains of an old log cabin (41) that belonged to Mar Perrine.

Perrine may have been the homesteader, but in 1921, the Morrow family bought the place and built the houses and barns that still stood in 1990. Next to Morrow's place is the Hamilton Hancock (sometimes spelled Hancox) homestead that was farmed in later years by Hancock's son-in-law, Burt Perrine. All that remained of the Perrine place in 1990 were remnants of a potato shed (42).

Julius Ramm had the next claim of 120 acres pursuant to a 1910 homestead patent signed by President William H. Taft. The place changed hands several

The remains of the Lester Holloway claim.. The farmstead grew over the years of successive owners such as the Bernbeck and Campbell families. (26)

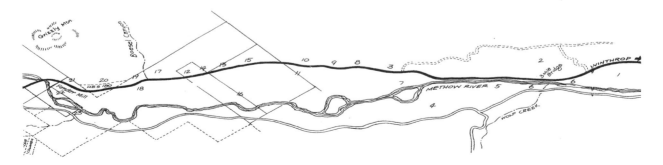

times but the little house (43) and barn which were on the land in 1990 were built by Dale Allen. Next door, Dale's father, Ed Allen, cleared the land and built the house that is known as "Brown's Farm" in the 1990s (44). Ed Allen was Lester Holloway's brother-in-law.

Over on Kumm Road, against the hill, was the original Lester Holloway place (26).

A little to the east, in the middle of the valley, at the end of Lucky Jim Road, is the spot where John McKinney staked his claim in the 1890s (25). Later, the Harry Briggs family homesteaded the site. Frank Kumm, Roy's father, bought the place from Briggs in 1924. Frank added to the house and Roy and Doris moved in after Frank's death. On January 16, 1957, in temperatures of 20 degrees below zero and with a fierce wind blowing, a chimney fire burned the house to the ground. The Kumms rebuilt that summer and it was remodeled in 1991.

Moving up the valley, next to Holloway was HES 181 (45), claimed by Paul Schenk. Holloway purchased this along with HES 182 in the early 1920s.

On the southwest corner of Highway 20 and Kumm Road was the

Flieschman place (46). The Flieschmans bought it in 1923 from the old bachelor homesteader named Clayton. The house and barn sat back near the mountain next to the willow trees. The house on Highway 20 (46a) was built in 1947.

Across the road was George Lintzmeyer's place (47). George built the

With Goat Peak as a background, the Lintzmeyer farmstead has been an active place for decades. Before the Rocking Horse riding stables, which have occupied the facility for the past decade, the Button family had a snowmobile race track on the grounds. (47)

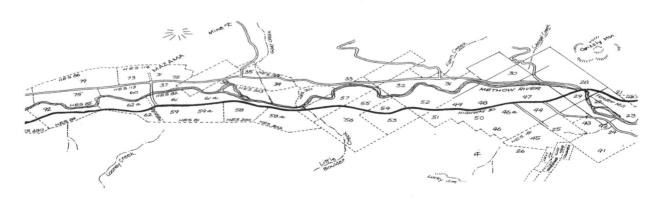

Motzkus house. (48)

house and barn that were still standing in 1990. In 1990, the place was known as the Rocking Horse Ranch. Prior to that, however, it was owned by the Button family who had built a snowmobile race track in 1969 in a large field by the road west of the house. They converted an outbuilding to a snack bar and scheduled competitions during the winter. Although the elaborate operation seemed like a good way to make use of the Mazama snow, it lasted only a few seasons.

The next house up the valley (48) was said to have been built by Bob Kifer, but it is not known who cleared the fields or

farmed the land. The John Motzkus family lived there for many years and raised hay for horses.

Next on the north side of the road lie the remains of an old barn built by Elbert Cassel (49).

The original house built by Howard Weller sat by the willow tree. It burned down and Elbert put a trailer there in later years. Elbert farmed, mined, logged, and even tried to run a trucking service to Mazama from down the valley. The barn was torn down in 1994.

The Elbert Cassel barn stood until the 1990s near the great weeping willow tree which was in the yard of the original house. (49)

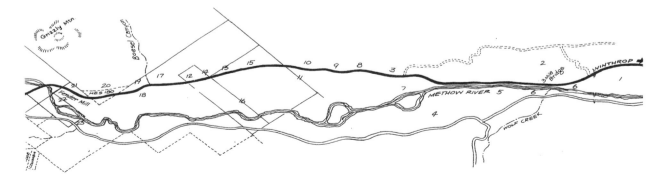

27

Across the road to the south lies a parcel which Bill Stewart originally bought from Wes Holloway. The house and barn that Bill occupied have long since vanished. Wes Holloway, Lester's brother, purchased the property and subdivided it into 40-acre plats (50).

Several houses sit here, on the southwest side of this stretch of road. The first house in the subdivision was said to have been built by Bob Scott and was occupied by Kenneth Dick in the 1950s.

The next farmstead contains a house and barn built by Floyd Kent (51). The Kent family lived there from 1931 until 1943.

The Charlie Bowers family bought a plat from Wes Holloway and in the 1930s built the two-story house, barn, and outbuildings that are still standing in the 1990s (53). Stan Dick built the little house just west of the farm. Stan cleared some of the field behind his house and raised hay. Stan sold to a developer who built a residential subdivision on the property.

Across the road from the Kents, on the northeast side, near

The one-room McKinney school, shown here after an early snow, was located across the road from the Kent home next to an apple tree which was still growing in 1996. (52)

The Bower's house and outbuildings include barns, a chicken coop, and a storage building that was moved in from the Mazama Queen mine in the 1950s when the Dick family occupied the place. (53)

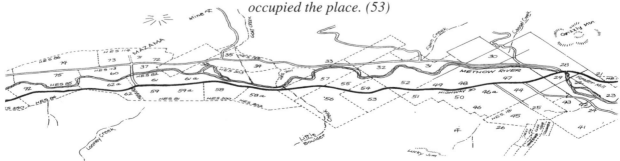

a lone apple tree which was still growing in 1996, was the site of the Mt. McKinney school (52).

Upriver a few hundred feet was a small house with a dirt floor, which stood until the 1970s, and had been the home of Napolean Bowes, a well-known character in Mazama from the 1940s to the mid-1960s. Napolean was brought into the valley by Andy Russell on one of Andy's trips hauling cattle to the coast. Andy picked up Napolean along the road where he was walking with rags tied around his feet for shoes. Andy and his wife fed Napolean and gave him clothes in return for his work.

Napolean became sort of a community ward, working here and there for food and a place to live. It was thought that he was of a mixed race because of his skin color and features, but Napolean wasn't sure where he was born (he thought maybe in West Virginia), how old he was, or who his parents were. No one knew if he could read or write. He seemed familiar with just about any place that had a railroad yard and spoke of living with the Indians, but other than that, he and his past were a mystery.

Eventually, Napolean settled into the job of changing sprinklers for Karl Duffy who owned several places around the Little Boulder Creek area. Karl would feed and clothe Napolean all year and provide him with firewood. When the Doug Devin family took over the Little Boulder Creek ranch, Napolean seemed to go with the land and the Devins continued the practice Karl had begun. Napolean would tell a neighbor what he wanted from the store, the neighbor would call it in to the grocery store, and the mailman would leave it by the side of the road. Napolean's bill was charged to the Devins, who never worried about Napolean taking advantage of them. Napolean was quite frugal. When he was given a new shirt or pants, he would put it on over his existing clothes and never took the old ones off. He had a stringy black beard and long black hair which he put into an alfalfa sack he used as a hat.

Both Karl Duffy and Doug Devin paid Napolean in cash. Doug tried to get Napolean to apply for a Social Security number, but he would have no part of it, saying, "a fellow ought to take care of hisseff." Doug finally got him to approve of a bank account and Napolean brought him $20 or $30 to deposit. Each bill was tightly rolled up into the shape of a matchstick. After this, Napolean's earnings

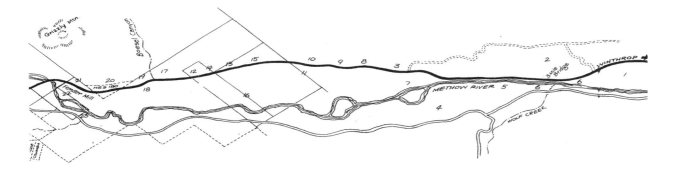

Napolean Bowes, on the right, helping Doug Devin fix a fence in about 1967. Napolean's hat is made from an alfalfa seed bag rolled up on the sides. He wore all the clothes he had ever been given, regardless of the temperature.

were put into the bank. After Napolean died, the sheriff went through his shack and reported finding about $1,800 in small bills hidden in sacks, cans, and old socks.

Nature seemed to look out for Napolean. He died of a heart attack before the winter of 1968. That winter, the temperature dropped to 50 degrees below zero, which would have been torture for Napolean in his dirt-floored shack.

Moving west, up valley from the present Liberty Bell subdivision, the next homestead was that of the Youngblood family (53). Bill Stewart remembered this area as having many very large fir trees that were specially logged for custom milling for the power house at Chelan Falls. The Fender Mill spent weeks on this job.

Robert Sloane had a 160-acre homestead which was located on both sides of today's road. On this section of the road, there are two houses on the north side. The first, built by Guy Wyscaver (54), is known by some as "Joybelle." The white house immediately adjacent to the highway (55) was built by Robert Sloane. Later, Andy Russell farmed it for a number of years. The Bible Camp next to Robert's place is located on land homesteaded by Lew Davis (56).

Mr. Wickert had the next homestead (57) which also crossed today's highway and stretched down to the river and across Little Boulder Creek. The house sat on the north side of the road. It burned to the ground in the 1960s and all that remains is a garden of beautiful poppies to brighten the landscape each spring.

On the south side of the road is the small white building which served as the

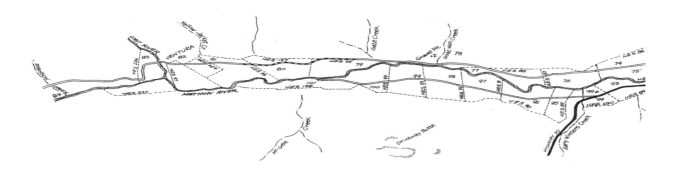

The Mazama Community Church occupied the old Crawley house, which had been moved from Little Boulder Creek. A new church was built down valley in 1986.

Bill and Martha Stewart's house in the 1980s after it had been abandoned for 10 years. At one time, the house was a "showplace" of Mazama with a neat white fence around a yard full of flowers. (58a)

Mazama Community Church for several years. The building had been moved from Little Boulder Creek near what in the 1990s is the entrance to the Devin ranch. The building had once been the home of the Wickerts' daughter who married a fellow named Crawley.

HES 202 was homesteaded by Robert Sloane's brother, Tom. Tom was Martha Stewart's father and he gave the west 40 acres of the property to Martha and Bill Stewart, where they lived for 50 years. The house (58a), barn, and chicken coop were still standing in 1996, but show little indication of the showplace home which once existed.

Tom Sloane had adjoining homesteads, HES 200 and HES 202. The latter was in the name of Nancy Sloane, Tom's mother. HES 200 went to Tom and then after Tom, Josh Graves owned the place and built the barn. Aaron Burkhart purchased it in 1958 (58).

Burkhart and his family farmed the entire tract until the 1990s and continued to farm a part of it after selling off some parcels to pay off debts.

Two early homesteads border the road adjacent to the present Mazama Road. On the south is HES 81 which was Harley Wehmeyer's place (59), and on the north was Fred Patterson's place, HES 82 (61). The story goes that Lou Wehmeyer,

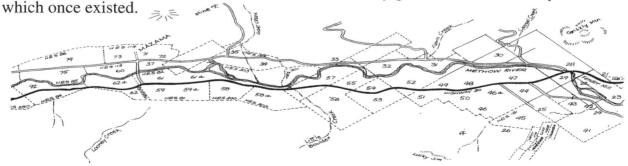

The Sloane homestead now owned and farmed by the Burkhart family. (58)

Harley's brother, filed on HES 82 but failed to "prove up" on the land and Fred Patterson got it, which made Lou and Fred bitter enemies for life. Harley later gave Lou 30 acres off the east side of his place, where Lou built the little house (59a) that still sat by the side of the road in 1990. On the east end of the Patterson place, a fellow named Jones built a little sawmill (61a) by the river which operated for about four years solely by sawing the logs off HES 82. Apparently, the Mazama area grew very fine trees.

On the south side of the highway where it joins with the Mazama Road is HES 83, which Will Looney homesteaded (62). Andy Russell had a few acres on the east side of HES 83 on which he raised chickens and a milk cow after he quit farming down the valley. He constructed a building from parts of a coffer dam on a Columbia River hydroelectric project. The Russells had a gas pump and cafe, and Mrs. Russell did the cooking. Called the Do Drop Inn, it lasted only a few years.

Karl Duffy mentioned that he didn't think the eating experience in the cafe was enhanced by the cafe's frequent visitor, Napolean. According to Karl, Napolean "smelled pretty

The Do Drop Inn.

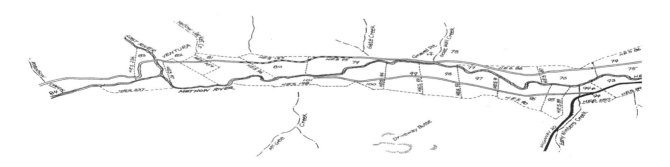

stout" inside a building. The property was also a collection spot for old iron for many years. Andy kept busy in his retirement collecting scrap iron and piling it in front of his house. The iron remained until the new highway right of way was established in 1970.

Mazama to Early Winters

Will Looney came to Mazama about the same time as his brother-in-law, Fred Patterson. They filed for homestead claims at the same time. Will got HES 83, which was next to Copper Mountain (now called Sandy Butte), and Fred took the spot by the river, HES 82 (61). In later years, Harvey Peters, a sawmill man, bought HES 83. Harvey and his son Ellis built a sawmill (62a) on the northeast side of the present State highway, opposite the barn. The Peters lived in a small cabin by the lower line and cut timber off their land. They made apple boxes in their shake mill and planner mill for the Nickell Brothers Packing House.

Ellis married Martha, a teacher who came to teach at Mazama and boarded with the Peters. Ellis and Martha started building their house in 1933 with lumber from their mill, and finished it in 1938, the same year the mill burned to the ground.

Ellis Peters' home. (62)

Next to Ellis Peters' place on the road to Early Winters Creek is HES 84, homesteaded by Albert Parkinson. Not much is known about Albert. In later years, Bill Fulton farmed the place and built a house and barn near the river in the same area where the present house is located (92). Bill's cabin was once the temporary home of the Mazama school. In the 1990s, the property is being operated as the Chokecherry Inn.

The next house (93) on the north side of the highway was built by Bob Wise, Ellis Peters' son-in-law.

On the south side of the road is HES 250, homesteaded by Loys Taylor and then purchased by Les Holloway. Les sold it to Jack Wilson who, in the late 1940s, started building the Early Winters Resort (94). Construction began with three

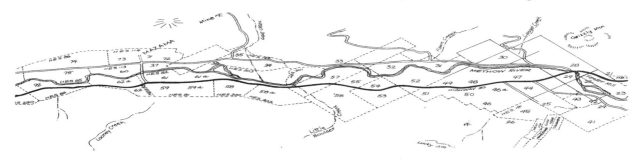

33

cabins right on the creek, a barn, and corrals. Jack then built four more cabins near the Early Winters ditch.

The original ford and county bridge crossed Early Winters Creek near the United States Forest Service ranger station at the northeast end of the present campground (94a).

Up the river from Early Winters Creek on what became known as Cassal Road, seven homesteads were cut out of the wilderness. This is a particularly beau-

This classic turn of the century style house was built by the homesteader, Louis VonDell. He was followed by the Warren Willis family, who sold the property to Len Miller. The Miller family farmed a little and raised Malamute dogs before they left and sold to the Early Winters resort development partners. (95)

tiful area, facing Goat Wall with a view from every angle. With the beautiful surroundings, however, went exceptional hardships for pioneers, including isolation, marginal soils, and three times as much snow in the winter as in nearby areas.

HES 89, the first claim next to Early Winters Creek, was the homestead of Louis VonDell. Louie was mostly a blacksmith, but he built the classic homestead house (95) which was barely standing in the 1980s, but was in the process of being preserved.

Not much is known about VonDell except information recalled from boyhood memories by his neighbor, Bud Short. VonDell ran a few cows and made his own wine. Wine making was probably motivated by economic concerns on VonDell's part, as he was known to consume wine in great quantities. His young neighbor, Bud Short, remembers seeing VonDell spill a glassful of wine on the table and then scoop it back into the glass with his dirty hand. The event made a lasting impression on young Bud.

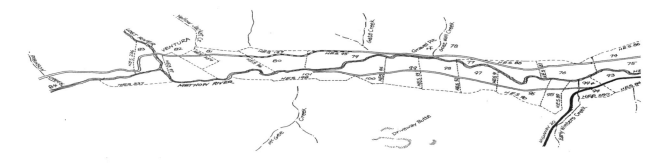

Bud also remembered that VonDell got a nail embedded in his foot, which became badly infected. Another neighbor, Harold Grant, had a Model-T Ford and drove VonDell to the hospital in Wenatchee to have his foot looked at. According to Bud, Louie "raised hell with the doctors and nurses" and claimed that his foot just needed to be "stomped on." VonDell would try to stomp around the hall of the hospital, only to have his foot get worse. The doctors and nurses finally got him on an operating table to amputate the foot. Unfortunately, however, VonDell died on the table. He is buried in Winthrop.

Warren Willis took over HES 89 and farmed after VonDell died. Willis remained there until the 1960s, at which time he sold the tract to the Len Miller family.

Bill Dunham had the next place, HES 90 (96), although the exact location of the house is unknown. Both HES 89 and 90 stretched from the mountain to the Methow River.

Alva Welch claimed HES 91 and built a house (97) and barn. Remains of the house are standing in 1990s, but the barn is gone. The house is sometimes referred to as the "Rattlesnake House" because a group of local children on horseback once saw a snake slink under the house. They spoke of the incident a number of times among themselves in the presence of others and the name caught on. It is true that snakes have been frequently seen in the area.

In about 1910, HES 92 was the homestead of William (Bill) Voight, who built a house and barn on the tract. (98) At the time the house *"was the only painted*

Bill Voight probably built this barn on HES 92 that the Short family used. Charlie Woods, a Mazama pioneer, on the right is aided by visiting friends putting up hay in the 1930s. (98)

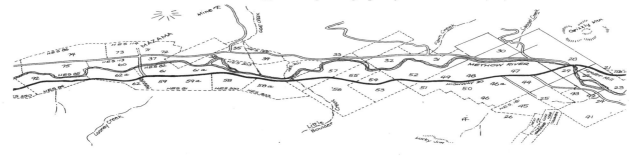

house in the valley, pink and white." The Short family bought the house in 1922. Ranson Short worked for the Great Northern Railroad and lived and worked in Wenatchee before buying HES 92. His family of three boys and two girls ran the farm. The oldest girl, Edith, married Harold Grant and they moved into the vacant house next door on HES 93.

Goat Wall School students pictured here when the school was located on the east side of the river on HES 88. Back row: Dwight Courier, Teacher Mildred McDermott, Alice Peters, Kenneth Courier, Earl Short, Bud Mays. Front Row: Carl Peters, Clara Courier, Bud Short.

The youngest Short child, Bud, was born the year after the Shorts moved onto HES 92. Bud grew up and lived on HES 92 until he left for World War II in 1942. He remembers going down the lane of trees at the end of the field to the "Black Bear Ford" which crossed the river by Goat Wall Creek. The school was located for a short time on the opposite side of the Methow. The children would cross the river on a big old fallen cottonwood tree. Soon, however, a one-room school was built on HES 94 on their side of the river to serve the Early Winters area children, and they no longer had to walk the log.

Members of the Short family lived on HES 92 as well as on HES 93 for many years. The remains of an assortment of farmstead buildings (98) exist today, but the house was moved from its original site up-valley a few hundred feet many years before Don and Dorothy Shafer bought the place in the early 1940s. The Shafers enlarged the fields and raised cattle on the land. They eventually owned HES 91, 92, and 93, and with their range permit, ran over 300 cows. The remains of an assortment of farmstead buildings (98) are all that are left of HES 92.

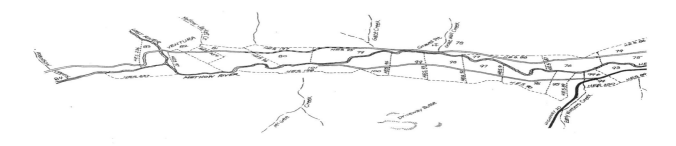

HES 93 was homesteaded by Dennis Overturf. He built part of the little house (99) that today lies in ruins at the upper end of Shafer Field. Dennis had some cows and his wife cooked in the boarding house in Mazama. Dennis died at a young age, and his wife and children could not pay the taxes on the place, and lost it. The Short family occupied the place later, before the Shafers.

Calloway Cassal claimed HES 94 and purchased HES 198 adjoining it on the upriver side. Calloway built his house (100) and barns, the majority of which are still standing and in use in the 1990s. The large barn on the level with the road was built from the large trusses which

Cassal farmstead. (100)

Calloway salvaged from the Green Mill and hauled across the river.

HES 198 had been homesteaded by John and Temperance Arnold who built a house (101) on the bank overlooking the river at the very upper end of the present field. The house burned and the family moved. John died and Temperance eventually lost the place to the bank. Calloway also eventually acquired HES 197, which extended to the other side of the river.

Cassal was an industrious fellow. His entire field was enclosed with a high deer fence to protect his hay crop. The story is told that Calloway had so much trouble with deer that he had to shoot large numbers of them. He would stack up the carcasses and call the Game Department to pick them up. After repeated occurrences of this and the payment of damages to Calloway, the Department felt it would be prudent to build a fence around the field, which was just fine with Calloway. The Department put the contract to build the fence out to bid and Calloway was the low bidder. Everyone was happy — Calloway had a well paying job building the fence, the Game Department was relieved of the task of picking up dead deer and paying damages, and the deer were not being shot.

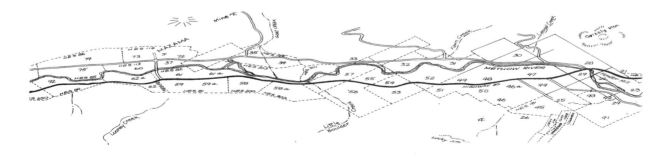

Mazama to Lost River on the Slate Creek Road

On the other side of the river heading toward Lost River from the Mazama Bridge is HES 114 on the right (northeast) side of the road. This was homesteaded by Ed Kagel and over the years was the site of many Mazama activities. Besides an early store and post office (71) located adjacent to where the community building is today (72), the Dan Lee Mine was located there for a short period of time. Considerable timber was taken off the land. Among others, the Stookey family farmed and improved the tract and built a house which stood for many years. Charlie Bowers bought the place and built the barn. Some of the other outbuildings were moved from the Mazama Queen Mine. After Bowers, the Eggleston family lived there and farmed the place. In the 1970s, a group of developers purchased and platted the property and built the Mazama Country Inn. In 1995, the old house and barn were converted to a new inn, the Mazama Ranch House.

In the 1940s, Bill and Vi Pederson built the Mazama Store and Post Office (73) on a portion of HES 114. Harold Bowers had sold Pederson an acre for $90 on which to build a post office and store. The post office had formerly been near what is now the southwest corner of the junction of Goat Creek and Lost River Roads. The Pedersons lived in a mobile home and the post office was inside the store. Bill kept adding on to the building as the business grew. After several owners and operators in the 1970s and 1980s, Jeff Sandine purchased the business and the buildings in the 1990s. Jeff demolished all the structures and built a large new store and post office. The post office, however, was short lived. Jeff could not put up with the red tape and the bureaucrats that accompanied running a post office, and he moved it out of the store after only a few months.

Up river from the Mazama Bridge on the left (southwest) side of the road was the homestead of Angus McLeod, HES 113. The next homestead was HES 85, claimed by Matt Heiderscheit. Across the road from Matt's was HES 86, claimed by Jeremiah Bader. Jeremiah sold his claim to Matt, making him the owner of a tract that stretched from the mountain to the river. Matt built a large three-story house (74) near the mountain, along with a barn and outbuildings.

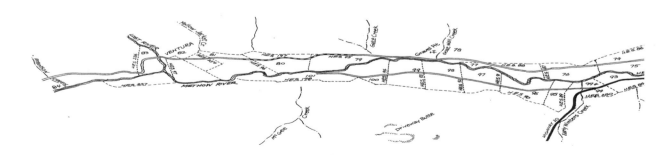

HES 86, Matt Heiderscheit's house, photographed in 1995. Matt had a herd of about 30 milk cows, one of the larger herds in the upper valley. Matt was a fine old German builder who helped build many homes in the valley, and at the bottom of Goat Wall, built a fine 3-story house with a barn and outbuildings. In typical Mazama soil conditions, Matt attempted to clear a field of stone for pasture, and gathered enough material to build a mound of stone along his fence line. (74)

Matt was a bachelor and was said to have been a good carpenter. Although he worked as a carpenter, he also kept thirty

milk cows. In later years, A.L. Thompson bought HES 85 on the river side of the road and subdivided the property into over thirty long, narrow tracts (75).

At this point on the road, the cliff is next to the road on the right and HES 87 is on the left, or river, side. Henry Countryman had the original claim on this land and later Jim Lewis held it. Jim built a barn (76), had a few cows, and "irrigated the rocks" to get some pasture. As Bill Stewart remembers, there were a few spots where Jim got "some pretty good hay." The place burned down in the 1950s because of careless hunters.

HES 88, located next to the river, was the home and claim of Guy Sharp. Guy cleared the place and farmed various crops, but what everyone remembers are Guy's big fields of cabbages. Guy made sauerkraut and sold it in town along with his cabbages. He was also an early "developer" and created Sharp Acres, a row of small tracts along the road to the left. Larry Higbee built some small houses on the tracts, and the area was called Prenticeville. Guy's house (77) stands by the big rock at the bottom of Goat Wall.

Here, the road runs at the base of Goat Wall for some distance. Just before Goat Wall Creek is the site of the Mazama Queen Mine (78) which ran off and on for

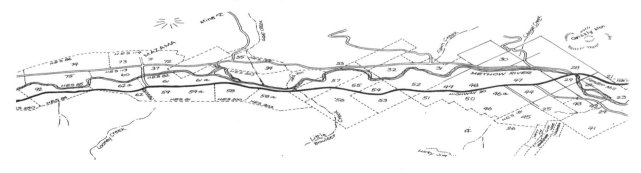

Several members of the Sharp family built homes in Mazama. This was the home of Guy Sharp with Last Chance Peak in the background. (77)

many years. The operation consisted of a mine high up on Goat Wall and a mill a few hundred feet off the road, and used water from Goat Wall Creek. At times, the mill hired as many as 40 to 50 men.

The next private property, HES 95, starts at Gate Creek and lies to the left of the road. It was claimed by Albert Boughey, who built a cabin (79) and worked away at the land enough to prove up his claim. Albert was best known in the community as a violin player. He sold to H.C. (Harvey) Peters who built a small sawmill on the property. Peters previously owned a mill down the valley next to the Mt. McKinney school.

After Peters, the property was taken over by Charlie Woods, who was known for his gardens. Charlie grew wonderful vegetables because the warmth of Goat Wall prevented frosts long after the rest of the valley's gardeners had lost their gardens for the season. In 1984 the Sitts' built a large log house and barn on the property and continued to raise a big garden aided by Goat Wall.

H.C. Peters also homesteaded the adjacent HES 197, which he later sold to Archie Green. Archie took over the sawmill business and built a mill on the property (80). In later years, after the mill had been taken out by a mud slide, Archie sold the property to Calloway Cassal.

HES 96 is the next place down the road. It appears that the land between HES 95 and HES 96 went unclaimed for a period of time. William Robinson homesteaded HES 96 and kept the land for many years. It is thought that William Robinson was not related to the Robinson brothers who originally had the camp on Robinson Creek and after whom the creek is named. There was a small 60-acre homestead claim taken out of the middle of the property in later years.

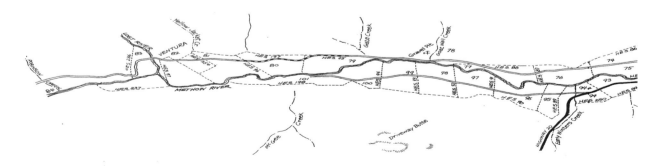

Bessie Hardy's fine house built with the help of Alvie Sharp is located on Lost River Road. It has been well taken care of and probably looks as good today as it did in Bessie's day, except that the attraction of Bessie is gone. (81)

On the right side of the road, before the road to Yellow Jacket Creek, is a nice house (81) with a stone foundation which was built by Alvie Sharp for his "friend" and, for a period, his wife, Bessie Hardy.

Bessie, known locally as "Lost River Bessie," ran a roadhouse which served chicken dinners. She was said to have sold Alvie's moonshine and her homemade brew, along with her favors, to the menfolk who passed by. Bessie was popular locally. She would occasionally be jailed for some infraction, such as delivering a carfull of moonshine to the Rockview Hall. Inevitably, a neighbor would show up the next morning and bail Bessie out of jail.

Just up river from Yellow Jacket Creek is an area known as Ventura, which served as a large tent city for Colonel Hart when he was building the Harts Pass Road. Speculation that a town would develop at this site was obviously quite premature, if not entirely incorrect.

HES 97 borders Lost River where it meets the Methow River and was claimed by Harry Mayfield who sold it to

Bessie Hardy in 1921.

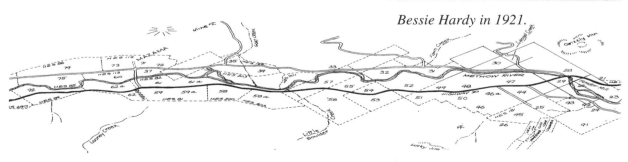

The home of Hazard and Zora Ballard at Lost River. (82)

river. In the 1960s, a restaurant known for its chicken dinners was located across the road toward the Methow River.

Across the Lost River Bridge lie the remains of a number of log houses. These were reported to have been used as a supply station for shipping to mines and as a base for the dog teams used to transport supplies and mail throughout the winter.

On the right side of the road after crossing Lost River is HES 236, a small homestead claimed by Edwin Farnam. Some say that the log cabin (83) right off the road was built by

Hazard Ballard. Harry had been active in the early days of the Slate Creek mines and at one time had the contract to carry the mail to Barron. Hazard had a pack string of forty animals and, in the early 1900s, ran a hotel in Robinson.

Up the Methow River from the Lost River Bridge is HES 237, claimed by Charles Mayes and later sold to Zora Ballard, Hazard's wife, after Hazard's death.

By the 1980s, part of HES 97 had become the site of the Lost River air strip and a large subdivision of vacation homes developed by "Pete" Arnold. Hazard's house (82) was located at the upper end of the property, where the road turns to go down to the

The Lost River area contains the remains of log buildings that are reported to be left from the days when dog teams serviced the Azurite mine in winter.

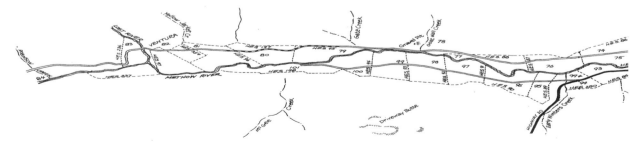

the Hudson Bay Company, but according to Bill Stewart, Edwin built it in the 1920s.

The road goes on to Robinson Creek, where in 1900 a post office and the Last Chance Saloon were located. (84) The facility served the sizable population of prospectors and men working on Harts Pass Road. For a short time, Guy Waring located one of his Methow Trading Company stores in Robinson to serve the min-ers headed for the Slate Creek mines. Why the land was not homesteaded is not known. In the 1930s, a large Civilian Conservation Corps, or CCC, camp was located at Robinson and remained there for several years. By the 1990s, no trace of any settlement remained. If one scrapes the dirt, however, an occasional piece of metal or a nail can be found, testifying to the existence of something on the site.

This picture was labeled as "Robinson" and could be the Last Chance Saloon and the Robinson Hotel, or it may be the Methow Trading Company store and the post office, or all of those.

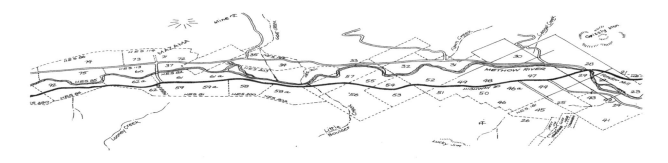

Part II - A Chronological Account of the Development in the Mazama Area

Chapter 1

First Records of Exploration of the Mazama Area

(Excerpts from *Northwest Discovery,* volume 4, June, 1983)

George Backus, George Goethals, A.M. McGee

First Lieutenant George Benjamin Backus (1851? - 1895), a 1871 graduate of West Point, led the detachment that was sent to explore the upper Methow. He had earlier accompanied the Pierce expedition in 1882 across the Kettle Range of the North Cascades.

First lieutenant George Benjamin Backus Jr., a native of Pennsylvania and a graduate of West Point, was 32 years old in the summer of 1883. He arrived at Osoyoos Lake with General Sherman's party on August 12 and was promptly ordered into the Methow country to explore and map the area and look for a pass through the Cascade Mountains. Protecting the northern frontier and facilitating settlement and economic growth were some of the federal government's objectives in finding a pass through the North Cascades. A party of miners claimed to know a route, and a route had been mentioned in a scouting party's report the previous year. Lieutenant Backus was part of this scouting party and knew about where the pass might be found if it really existed.

Lieutenant George Washington Goethals was ordered to accompany the party on the search for the pass. Lieutenant Backus commanded Lt. Goethals to make maps and record the events of the trip. Goethals would go on to become a professor of engineering at West Point and be appointed by President Theodore Roosevelt to replace John Stevens (who discovered Stevens Pass) as chief engineer and the first American Governor of the Panama Canal.

The exploration party consisted of six men, including Backus and Goethals; *"a saddle animal for each man; four pack mules; and one hound dog."* The party left

First Lieutenant George Washington Goethals (1858 - 1928) was second in command of the expedition and wrote the report for the party submitted to the Engineering Office of the U.S. Army, Department of the Columbia. Goethals would go on to distinguish himself and gain the attention of Secretary of War William Taft, who recommended him to Theodore Roosevelt as the chief engineer of the Panama Canal. He was later promoted by Act of Congress directly from colonel to major-general, and from 1914 to 1916 served as the first American governor of the Canal Zone.

Osoyoos Lake the morning of August 15, 1883, and proceeded along the Similkameen River.

This country was Indian land under Executive Orders of 1879 and 1880, which set aside a large tract of land roughly bordered by Lake Chelan, the Stehekin River, the Okanogan River, the Cascade Crest, and the Canadian border as an Indian Reservation for Chief Moses and the Columbia River Indians. The area was popularly known as "Moses' Reserve." However, what could be created by proclamation could be abrogated just as easily by proclamation. Thus, by virtue of an Executive Order issued by President Chester A. Arthur in 1883 and another issued in 1886 by President Grover Cleveland, the entire reservation was abolished and opened to white settlement and mining claims. This, of course, included the Methow Valley.

Lieutenant Backus had been to the Methow the previous year with the Pierce exploring party and was aware of the following entry made in the journal of one of the members of the expedition:

"At the foot of the ascent [at War Creek], I came with my Indian guide [Swa-u-lum] upon an old miner and his younger comrade cooking their noon-day meal of mountain goat's meat. They begged me to spare them a little flour, of which they were nearly destitute, in exchange for a shoulder of mountain goat. The request was granted much to their relief, when the train was unpacked that evening, and henceforth they clung to us for companionship to the very top of the Cascade range where

bewilderment, uncertainty of the locality and the loss of their strongest pack-horse down the rocks turned them homewards a disappointed pair."

The older of the two miners mentioned in the journal entry was probably A.M. McGee, who claimed to have lived in the mountains for thirty-two years, the last seven in this area, and appeared to be well informed on the country and the Indians. McGee reported that
"on one fork of the Methow River which headed opposite the Frazier River [actually he probably meant Slate Creek and the Skagit River] is a valley [the Methow Valley] unoccupied by whites,"
which he regarded as the finest he had seen east of the mountains for stock and grain.
"This river [the Methow] ascends to the summit [Harts Pass] from the south east by an easy grade, the elevation at the summit is much less than by the Snoqualmie route, and if the descent to the northwest is as gradual as on the east, it would form the best pass in the Cascade range for a wagon and railroad."

McGee reported that he *"went to the summit, nearly, in the month of January last [1877] and found no snow except on the north hill side."* He was sure, almost at least, that this pass was unknown to whites. It was this report from McGee as to the existence of a feasible pass somewhere north of Cascade Pass that prompted the U.S. Army Department of the Columbia to conduct further explorations.

Another report, however, would indicate that McGee was not the only white man to venture into this area. In the spring of 1880, a man named Dick Miller and his party came through from the Skagit headed for the Ruby Creek mines and camped at Early Winters, waiting for the high water to go down.

In late August, 1883, Lieutenant Backus came very close to meeting with the prospector McGee on the upper Twisp River. At the foot of the mountain, the Backus party passed a deserted camp which had recently been made, and since a horse shoe had been found along with pieces of clothing scattered about, they knew the camp had been made by a white man. They learned from some Indians upon returning to the Twisp that two white men had gone along the trail before them. From the description, Lt. Backus recognized the two miners from the year before.

When the Backus party returned from their exploration of the Twisp River it was September 1, 1883. Goethals recorded in his journal the following:

"Two days' march from the forks over the old trail, brought us to the Methow at the mouth of the Twotsp [the Twisp], where camp was made and a delay of two days made, partly for the benefit of our animals, partly to negotiate for the hire of a pony. Crpl. Rheinhardt had walked for the past four days, and his horse seemed to be getting worse. We succeeded in getting a pony and left the Corporal's horse to the cure of a 'medicine man' until our return."

Goethals's September 4, 1883, entry reads:

"From our camp here we followed the Methow on the right [southwest] bank in a general north-west direction for two days making in all 20 miles. An Indian whom we met near the end of our first day's journey warned us against proceeding too far on the trail, as marshes would be found [about 3 miles beyond the mouth of Wolf Creek] to stop our progress and return would be necessary, that portion of the trail was used by Indians only for hunting purposes."

Camp for the night of September 4 was two or three miles northwest of the mouth of Wolf Creek, "on a small stream whose course is parallel to the main stream, and which sinks a few hundred yards below where we were located."

The party continued to ascend along the southwest side of the Methow in a northwest direction. The next day, Goethals wrote:

"We crossed the creek on which our camp was located and ascended a small hill 175' then following a small valley for about three miles, we came again to the Methow, again going along the rest of the day by a well marked Indian trail."

Goethals's map shows that his party crossed Little Boulder Creek and made camp about one mile beyond Little Boulder and about two miles below the mouth of Early Winters Creek in what is today the community of Mazama. The entry of September 6, 1883 reads:

"About three miles beyond Camp [Mazama] we crossed a large tributary [Early Winters Creek]. We determined to turn westward and fol-

low this branch to its head. The Indians call this the 'Papoose Methow'."

Camp for September 6 was on the north side of Early Winters Creek, immediately above the confluence of Cedar Creek. The next entry, on September 9, 1883, states:

"We pushed forward the three miles the following day and camped just below the confluence of Papoose Methow [and probably Silver Star or Cutthroat Creek]. Before long a heavy rain set in which lasted all night and until late the following afternoon which forced us to remain in camp. Our only shelter was a fly of a wall tent that Mr. Chapman had brought for his own use for when we left the main party at Osoyoos we could get nothing in the way of a tent."

Towards evening on September 10, the storm passed and the air was once again clear. Lt. Goethals wrote that he and his men were

"thankful as we had been passing through smoke ever since we left the head of the north fork of the Twotsp. We could see ahead of us the snow covered zigzag peaks resembling those at the Northfork of the Twotsp, and which did not appear a great distance off. We decided to camp another day for plenty of good grazing could be had."

The next day, the party started for the summit without a pack train and was gone all day. Although Lt. Goethals's map depicts a small portion of Early Winters

Creek above the confluence of Cutthroat Creek, Lt. Backus at this juncture chose to ascend Cutthroat Creek instead of Early Winters. His reason for doing so is probably because he was seeking a route and pass westward to the Skagit. Cutthroat Creek led him to the southwest, whereas upper Early Winter Creek headed in a due south direction. As a consequence of his choice, Backus's action led him to a cul-de-sac and he missed the opportunity to discover easy Washington Pass, which now is the North Cascades Highway. Backus's misjudgment is understandable, however, since the east side of Washington Pass is so well hidden that one must ascend to the absolute head of Early Winters Creek before the pass becomes visible.

Lieutenant Goethals's last entry regarding Early Winters states:

"For those who are now desirous of going up that stream it would be well for them to follow our route as shown by the blazed trees, but they should not follow it with the attempt of getting across the Cascade Range. For hunting purposes the country is certainly a good one."

Chapter 2

The 1890s - Mining Interests Flourish

Since the 1870s, miners had been prospecting up Ruby Creek, a tributary of the Skagit River, and they eventually reached Slate Creek. Alex Barron's discovery of the Eureka lode in 1893 started a gold rush. The camp and town which developed were appropriately called Barron. To reach Slate Creek from the west was a grueling effort and some found it downright hair-raising. Miners eventually found the eastern approach through the Methow to be easier than the western route.

In March of 1895, Colonel W. Thomas Hart came into the Methow with resources at his disposal and took options on mines at Squaw Creek and in the Slate Creek district. Colonel Hart was reported to be "corpulent and courtly." Despite his title of Colonel, however, there was no evidence that the Georgia-born mining man and promoter had ever been associated with the Confederate army. There was no record of his name in a listing of officers, but bestowing military titles upon oneself was a common practice after the Civil War, regardless of the minor detail of whether one actually served in the military or not.

Colonel Hart managed or "experted" the Eureka Mine, which had been prospected a few years earlier. The mine became a big producer. Tons of equipment and supplies to support the mine were taken up through Mazama and Robinson on crude trails by pack animals. Colonel Hart engaged Charles H. Ballard to survey a road along the north side of the Upper Methow River, crossing the summit at what was then known as Slate Pass, soon to be re-named Harts Pass. By mid-April of 1895, Hart had sixty-five men working out of a camp in Ventura, about a half mile downriver from Lost River, on a narrow gauge wagon road starting at Lost River. The road climbed past Deadhorse Point, from which exposure an entire string of pack horses and the packer (who survived) were said to have plummeted a thousand feet almost straight down.

During the first week of June, after only two months of road building, Hart abruptly paid off his men and departed for Arizona. He had been *fired by his syndicate,"* said the *Leavenworth Times. "Extravagant and unnecessary use of money [caused] Col. Hart's tumble from the pinnacle of prominence and power."* It is uncertain how far Hart had built the road. At its narrowest, the road was 26 inches wide, requiring wagons to be cut down and horses to be hitched in tandem. Apparently the Ballard brothers, Charles and Hazard, widened the road to 36 inches and completed it to the summit and down into Slate Creek.

Between 1893 and 1895, the Washington Territorial Legislature, pressured by mining interests, appropriated $30,000 and established a commission for a highway from Puget Sound to Marcus (an early mining and railroad center located north of Kettle Falls) in Eastern Washington. A reconnaissance party was sent up the Skagit and Slate Creek to Harts Pass. From there, the party traversed down Trout and Rattlesnake Creeks to the Methow. A second route under consideration was Thunder Creek from the Skagit, and a third was a Rainy Pass route which, although lower with an easier grade, was the longest and would require expensive rock excavation in the Skagit gorge.

This study was started on July 22, 1893, and in just fifty days the commission had completed and adopted the report. The commission ultimately decided that the shortest and most feasible route was from the Twisp River over Twisp Pass, down Bridge Creek, then up the Stehekin (at the head of Lake Chelan) and over Cascade Pass near Marblemount. The report recommending the Cascade route established the road width at 40 feet and ordered work to start in the spring of 1896. Obviously, governmental decision making was much more expeditious in the 1890s than it is today.

Work on the mountain part of the road was done by day labor under the supervision of the commission. The laborers' daily wage was $2.00 and the foreman's was $2.50. Board and room at the five camps was 75¢ per day. Because of the limited money, work was done without a survey except at a few critical points. In areas of heavy excavation, only a four-foot width was graded. Brush and timber were cleared to a width of 16 feet, and rocks and stumps were cleared from the roadway to allow wagons to pass.

Bridges were built where needed. Crews completed the entire road except for a small amount of brush-clearing along Bridge Creek before a heavy snow forced them to leave.

The commission was very proud of what it had accomplished in 1896, and felt it especially good from a national defense viewpoint. It reported that the wagon road provided a *"continuous highway for the movement of troops in case of necessity and particularly in protection of the northern frontier."* In testimony to what had been done, the commission reported that George Rouse, a local miner, rode horseback from the mouth of the Twisp River to the summit of Cascade Pass in one day and a few hours of the next, a distance of 53 miles. This was more than twice as fast as the former travel time.

The Legislature appropriated $21,000 the next year for further improvement and an additional six miles of roadway. However, when the crews could get into the high mountains they found that spring run-off had undone much of their work of the previous year. Slides and floods had washed out bridges and sluiced away long sections of the narrow grade. Repair work took all the money that had been appropriated and no further construction was possible that year.

The road was completed in 1899. The commission report called it *"a good road for mountain country"* over which *"four ordinary horses can pull 30 hundredweight (of freight) with ease."* Six years later, however, Joseph Snow, the first highway commissioner, characterized the result of all this work as *"a horse trail*

Guy Waring's Methow Trading Co. in the gold rush town of Barron.

from Marblemount to the summit of the Methow Range and about 12 miles of wagon trail down the Twisp River."

Regardless of all the efforts to construct a highway, the miners didn't benefit. Travel to the boom town of Barron and to the Slate Creek area was up the Methow past Robinson, around the narrow ledge and wooden platform hung on the side of Dead Horse Point, and over Harts Pass. For men, machines, and all their supplies, this supply line was open all year. Snow shoes and dog teams were used in winter and horses and mules the rest of the time.

———————

Meanwhile the Upper Methow was being settled. Hazard Ballard, brother of mining engineer, Charles, established his homestead at Lost River. Guy Waring's Methow Trading Company was doing business up and down the valley with upper valley posts in Barron, Robinson, Winthrop, and Twisp. At the peak of the boom in this area, when Hart was building the road to Slate Creek, there were 1,200 people in the Robinson and Lost River areas.

When Guy Waring, founder of Winthrop and the Methow Trading Company, first came in the spring of 1891, there were already a few settlers in the area, some at Rockview about seven miles above the site of Winthrop, and a few settlers downstream at Sullivan's flat. Waring established his squatter's rights on September 29, 1891, at the point where the Methow and Chewuck Rivers meet. Waring and his family spent their first fall in a tent. The cold weather was already settling in, and they not only cooked their meals on a stove, but also ate them from the stove to keep the food from freezing while they were eating it. In the old western tradition, neighbors soon arrived to help the Warings build their first house.

The following spring, 1892, "The Governor," as Waring was called by his family, put up a store, which was the beginning of the Methow Trading Company. The Warings had brought enough supplies and merchandise with them to stock the small store. His prices were notoriously high, but the early settlers were happy to have the convenience of a store in the upper valley. Waring was eventually appointed postmaster.

Winthrop circa 1894.

The winter of 1892-93 was extremely hard, with deep snow and bitter cold. On March 1, 1893, the Winthrop fire destroyed everything in the town. A twelve by fourteen foot root cellar was all that survived of the Warings' place. It served as the only store and post office in Winthrop. The Warings spent several weeks in a sixteen by twenty foot cabin across the river waiting for roads to open. As soon as travel was possible, Waring headed east seeking financial backing. Earl Johnson operated the business while Waring spent the next three years in the East raising money.

During the time the Warings were away, many changes took place in the area. In late winter of 1894, the local people built a bridge over the Methow River at the North Fork. The proud community had barely started to use their new bridge when it was washed out in the terrible flood of 1894 which wreaked havoc up and down the Methow, wiping out the town of Silver below Twisp. In 1895, the year after the high water carried away the bridge over the North Fork at Winthrop, the bridge was rebuilt by Colonel Hart on his march to the Slate Creek mining district.

The Warings returned in 1896 with enough financial backing to rebuild the store and expand the Methow Trading Company from Barron to Pateros. Winthrop was now quite a busy town with a blacksmith shop, a drug store, a hotel, and a little schoolhouse on the bluff. The big room on the second floor of the Methow Trading Company gave the community a place to meet and hold social functions and was the scene of many festive affairs.

Prospectors and miners, particularly those from the upper valley, were the main patrons of these Methow Trading Company stores. The Company patented the townsite of Winthrop ten years after it established its first store in Winthrop, and became the town's first real estate developer.

Around 1895, Charles Ballard, Hazard's brother, located the Mammoth Mine in the Barron area and managed it for years. More than Colonel Hart, it was Charles Ballard who became the prominent mining figure in the Methow and promoted the Azurite Mine in later years. Charles was, among other things, a civil and mining engineer. He eventually located in Twisp, but before coming to the Methow had laid out the towns of Chelan, Conconully, Oroville, and others. He filed

Guy and Elizabeth Waring in 1917 at their home in Winthrop, which is now the Shafer Museum.

the original plat for Chelan in 1889 when Okanogan County went from "the British line" to the Wenatchee River and Waterville was the county seat. Charles was the probate judge because he was one of the few well-educated men in the county.

———————

Early in the 1890s, a mine known as the Red Shirt Mine was discovered between Bensen Creek and Beaver Creek. Soon after the discovery, a mining engineer from England by the name of Jack Stewart came into the valley and purchased the mine. Stewart built a small reduction plant and put a crew of men to work. All went smoothly for a few years.

However, it apparently did not pay because Stewart suddenly dropped the mine and moved up to what was known as Goat Creek near Mazama. He and his company made a deal for the Flagg prospect. He put in a tramway from the mine down to a small reduction plant and set up a flume from Goat Creek for power.

Things worked well for several years until one day disaster struck. One of the loaded cars on the tramway near the mine broke loose. It ran down the track until it reached the plant and, with its heavy load giving it momentum, drove completely through the plant, killing two men who were working in the mill. Its speed was so great coming down the track that it curled the track right up behind the cars. The mine was closed for a number of years and Stewart moved the mine equipment to Slate Creek. After a few years, Stewart returned to Mazama and settled down, farmed, and became one of the first Mazama citizens.

———————

By the late 1890s, mining in the Methow had slowed. The Klondike gold rush of 1897-98 drained most of the miners from the valley. However, the areas between Winthrop and Slate Creek were beginning to fill with homesteaders and squatters. Albert Ventzke settled a few miles west of Winthrop. In 1892, W.H. Wehmeyer came into the country and homesteaded at Rockview. Wehmeyer's brother-in-law, Hank Johnson, settled next to him on his side of the river and started a small sawmill.

John McKinney

John McKinney was a Civil War veteran from Phillips County, Kansas, looking for work in the town of Demersville, Kansas. There wasn't any work, and he had been sitting around for almost a week. He kept a diary, and on Monday, January 8, 1892, he made the following entry: *"...being no stock to work with nor will not be for 2 or 3 weeks, I conclude to go to Washington and hunt up a homestead."*

McKinney spent the next ten days traveling around getting ready and sending some freight. On Thursday the 18th, he entered the following in his diary: *"8:30 a.m., jump freight train for Spokane. Fare $2 to ride 125 miles. Ride all night."*

On February 3, 1892, McKinney took the stage to Wenatchee and started his search. His diary describes the first of a number of walking journeys which would be considered marathons by modern standards, but were routine walks for McKinney at the turn of the century. He walked sixteen miles up the Wenatchee River and found snow a foot deep, then walked ten miles downriver and spent the night. The next day he walked back to Wenatchee and crossed the river on the ferry. The following day he walked all the way to Waterville where he met with some chums to compare notes on land they had seen. He then walked to Badger Mountain to look at a claim, which he ended up not liking.

During the next two days, McKinney walked twenty-four miles up the Okanogan River and stayed with a Mr. Malott. Over the next six days, he worked his way up the Methow. One night, he put up at Mason Thurlow's home, another at a Mr. Sullivan's house, and another at the Ventzke brothers' place, all the while looking for a claim he liked. On the 23rd of March his diary had this entry: *"Go 3 miles up the river to Mr. Hancock's. Snow too deep to hunt land in timber."* This would be the spot on which McKinney eventually settled. But for the time being, he returned to the Ventzke brothers' place and recorded that he moved onto Wolfe's ranch and operated out of there or "sat around camp." (The owner of Wolfe's ranch may have been the namesake of Wolf Creek, although this is not known for sure.)

Finally on April first, the following entry appears in McKinney's journal: *"Together with Mr. Hancock, Mr. Williams and T. Wolfe, we pace off my claim, lying west of Mr. Hancock's."* His claim was on the spot that Lt. Backus had probably stopped nine years earlier to water his horse. After staking the claim, McKinney immediately went to work laying foundation stones and poles for his cabin. The claim had level land, ponds, beaver dams, and lots of timber.

According to the diary entries during the period after the claim was staked, McKinney was a whirlwind of construction activity. On Sunday, he started his cabin and *"cleaned out the spring and fixed it up with stone, then cut brush at head of pond."* Starting on Monday, in three days he had cut a good wagon road 300 yards to his pond, finished his cabin and roof, put in a door and window, built a bunk and filled it with spruce and balsam feathers, and planted a garden with potatoes, carrots, turnips, rutabagas, and sunflowers. On the third day, the diary contains two short entries that were surely satisfying to John McKinney to write: *"Move into my cabin. Go to bed in my own home."*

McKinney's cabin remains on the farm that was later occupied by the Briggs and then the Kumm families. It is near the flowing spring that is the source of Hancock Creek. This is probably McKinney's second cabin judging from the description in his diary. (25).

The day after McKinney first slept in his own cabin, his diary shows that he started at 7:00 a.m. for the town of Ruby to look for work. It was a two-day walk and he arrived at 4:30 p.m. on Friday. But McKinney was unsuccessful in finding work. His diary records that he wandered to "Loomiston" (Loomis), Conconully, and Palmer Lake, and sat around camp for the next ten days. On Sunday he wrote, *"Still looking for work. Get box and fit up a shoe bench with milk cans for pegs and nails*

and commence sorting them out as they got mixed en route."

It wasn't until the first of May that McKinney finally found work building a boarding house for a stamp mill company. The work lasted for only two weeks, and on May 15, he headed back to the Methow to resume work on his place. He got back on Friday, according to the diary, in time to help his neighbor, Hancock, put up his kitchen. Back in the Methow, McKinney, a leatherworker as well as a general handyman, went into the shoe repair business. However, he was not a young man when he came into the country and the hard life and maybe the miles of walking took its toll. In 1902 or 1903, McKinney decided he needed care and was on his way to an old soldier's home on the coast when he was found dead near the depot in Wenatchee.

The spring and little creek that flow into the Methow from McKinney's place are now called Hancock Spring. The mountain that rises above his place is named McKinney Mountain, and the whole area is called the McKinney Mountain area. Although McKinney probably never had actual title to the land, he was well respected in the community and considered a homesteader.

Chapter 3

The 1900s and 1910s - An Economy Develops

With the turn of the century, more settlers began to arrive and the area became more than just a stopping place for miners bound for the Slate Creek mining area. Guy Waring's Methow Trading Company store in Barron was slowing down (it closed in 1905) and the mining boom at Slate Creek had ended. Prospecting, tunneling, and digging would continue to progress, although at a slower pace, on and off for the next fifty years. Waring was paying more attention to activities in the valley and, in addition to owning the Methow Trading Company, he was also the postmaster at Winthrop.

On October 28, 1900, at Waring's request, an application was prepared for the Robinson Post Office. It was to be located nine and a half miles northwest of Mazama, 13 miles southeast of Barron, and directly on Star Route 71382, which was to begin operation between Winthrop and Barron on November 15, 1900. The population to be served by the Robinson Post Office was listed as ten in the winter and fifty in the summer. The office was at a lumber camp and was the last stop before going over Harts Pass.

Business in Robinson, Mazama, and Rockview continued. The establishment of a newspaper in Twisp, the *Methow Valley News*, allowed for commercial advertising. For example, on January 1, 1904 the advertisement below appeared.

Within two years, however, the proprietor of the hotel had changed. The advertisement still ran in the paper, but Hazard Ballard, the new proprietor, added that the hotel was a *"Sportsman's Paradise"* and was located on the *"Slate Creek Route."*

On June 1, 1900, just a few months before the Robinson Post Office was established, Mrs. Minnie Tingley established the Mazama Post Office. The area now known as Mazama had originally been called Goat Creek by the residents in reference to the creek that flowed southward around Goat Peak. For some unknown reason, however, the Postal Service would not accept the name Goat Creek or

Winthrop started to look like a town in the 1900s. This picture shows a substantial bridge over the river and, at the left center, the irrigation canal behind the established original Duck Brand Saloon. In 1996, the building was the Town Hall.

Goat Mountain. At the suggestion of Guy Waring, the town was named "Mazama." Waring explained that Mazama was the Greek word for mountain goat. Actually, however, the word was a Latin or Spanish word for a wild horned animal, but that was close enough.

The mail came to the little post office in Minnie's home, a red three story house on HES 203, twice a week, by hack and horse in summer and by sleigh and horses in winter. Minnie would tie each patron's mail into bundles so that when someone came in on snowshoes, he would be able to deliver to others along the way. She always had a bowl of hot soup to serve to the mail carriers before they started on

the return trip. After a few years, Minnie found it necessary to give up the post office in order to care for her mother. She recommended Angus McLeod to succeed her as postmaster. Angus lived half a mile up valley from Minnie on HES 113 and kept an inn. Angus was chosen to succeed Minnie and ran the post office for the next fifteen years.

As evidenced by the preceding accounts, many of the original homesteaders and home builders in the Mazama area were miners. F.F. Ventzke was a civil engineer involved in mining. So were his brothers, Albert and Emil. Hazard Ballard came to the area to make his fortune in mining the Slate Creek

Stores at —

PATEROS – TWISP – WINTHROP – BARRON, WASH.

M. T. Co.'s Sawmill
AT ROCKVIEW

Rough Lumber now ready

Planed Stock, Lap Siding and Shingles will soon be a regular product

This 1903 advertisement for lumber could have been for a mill near Boesel Creek. The ad appeared before the Rockview Mill started.

area and became rich more than once on the mines. He was poor between his rich spells, however, and was also a packer.

———————

By 1910, several communities were emerging in the upper valley, with Robinson and Lost River at the head of the valley west of Mazama. McKinney Mountain was on the southwest side of the river. Rockview, across on the northeast side of the river, was home to an active sawmill. As settlers continued to arrive, more and more land was cleared and houses were built.

The Rockview Mill was located by the river on the Johnson homestead, known in later years as the Cooper place(16).

Lumbering became a major industry, and the Methow Trading Co. was selling lumber from a mill in Rockview.

In February of 1910, a firm composed of R.E. Johnson and H.I. (Hazard) Ballard bought the machinery from a sawmill at Chelan and moved it to Rockview. For about eighteen months the partnership operated as Johnson & Ballard, then Hazard bought out his partner (who was to become his father-in-law). Business was good at the mill and by September, 1912, Ballard was

Rockview Mill workers in about 1912. Left to right: Bill Jones, Berth Wehmeyer, Joe Ebbert & Genevieve, Roma Johnson, Dennis Overturf (or Will Thurlow), Harvey Lyons, Lou Wehmeyer.

planning to get bigger machinery. The week of September 12 it was reported that *"For the past week about 25 teams a day have been hauling lumber from the mill,*

The Winthrop paper in its second year of publication told about the importance of the creamery to the upper valley, had a story about a man being chased by a bear, and listed all of the people who checked in at the Forks Hotel from out of the valley. It is noteworthy that the pronunciation of the word "Methow" was a problem as early as 1913.

communications in the upper valley. Rockview was an active community and the paper carried notices and announcements of the activities in the area. For example, notices were published of a special election held to determine the site for a new school, the Rockview Grange's Monday meetings, and the dance on December 15 with music to be furnished by the Sanstrom Orchestra. The *Journal* also reported on practice games between the Winthrop and Rockview basketball teams. One game ended in a 17 to 15 victory for Winthrop. Basketball was played during the winter while the Rockview Mill was closed.

With the coming of spring in 1913, the decision on the location of the new Rockview school had been made. It was decided that *"one of those modern*

but on hand are hundreds of thousands of feet in the yard."

Neighbors in the Mazama areas began work on the Early Winters ditch about 1909 to get water down valley for irrigation on fields that were being logged and converted to crops. Meanwhile, in Winthrop, William Brinkerhoff purchased the defunct *Eagle Newspaper* and began publishing the *Methow Valley Journal* in 1912. The paper became a great aid in

The Methow log drive.

Although it was called a Winthrop band, its members were all from the upper valley and many played a role in the development of the Mazama area. Left to right: First row: W.E. Singer, Mose Brinkerhoff, Ferd Haase, Charlie Walters. Second row: Si Walter, Edgar Allison, Ferd Haase Sr., Reuben Hotchkiss, Carl Boesel, Alva Sharp. Top row: Amos Stokes, Andy Hall, Bill Haase, Roma Johnson, Al Haase.

schools would be erected." The lumber for the new $13,000 school would come from the local mill.

By June, 1913, Hazard Ballard had completed a very successful log drive of over a million feet of logs down the river to his mill in Rockview. The run started when the river was up from the spring melt, but this year because of a spell of cool weather the water fell again and handling the huge logs was very difficult in the low water. But, in credit to the mill workers' hard work, only one serious jam occurred. The jam was loosened with two cases of dynamite, and in total, the mill lost only about 2,000 feet of logs in the mishap.

On the social side, the *Journal* reported that the Fourth of July in Winthrop was:

"a gala day long to be remembered. . . Early in the morning people began to assemble for the interesting program. At 10:30 the Winthrop band appeared on the street and marched to Riverside Park. Rev. Berg started with a speech then the band played again before dinner.

"A number of tables were provided and the feast was spread featuring yellow-legged chicken. In the

PM the crowd was called together by the band for races. First of these was the nail-driving contest for ladies, then the muddle race. After this the crowd proceeded to the ball park for the finest exhibition of ball playing ever seen on the grounds. The married men took on the bachelors and defeated them 5 to 3. After the game there were the following contests: sack race, egg race, balance pole, ring riding. Then followed the Grand Ball by the band and the fireworks were numerous. Music for the dance was furnished by the Stokes orchestra which went till 12 o'clock."

Growth was continuing in Mazama. The *Methow Valley News* of June 14, 1912, reported that *"settlers up the West Fork of the Methow are building a wagon bridge across Early Winters Creek. This will be a great convenience as there is a long period each year that this stream cannot be forded."*

Harvey Peters arrived in the upper valley in 1912 and filed on an abandoned homestead (above Gate Creek on HES 197), built a log cabin, and started a sawmill. Bill Robinson had told Peters about the place being abandoned and later, Ellis, Harvey's son, found a stash of old sixty-gallon lard cans filled with dishes, bedding, and other personal effects on the property. Up on the hill behind the place was a mine digging and a log cabin with a rifle leaning against the wall, and no evidence that anything had been disturbed. Ellis never knew who the homesteader was

or what happened to him, but speculated that he might have been attacked by a bear or cougar. Harvey Peters sold the sawmill in 1919 to Archie Green and went back to West Virginia. He returned to the area in 1925.

After Jack Stewart quit mining, he built this barn, typical of New England barns, but unique to the Methow. The barn stood until it burned down in the 1960s (32).

A little less than a mile east of Mazama, on HES 203 (in the 1990s the Foster place), Jack Stewart was improving his homestead. Besides marrying Minnie, the postmistress, he erected a barn that attracted considerable attention. The barn was circular with a big silo in the center. While such barns were common in the East, they were unknown in this area. The barn was impressive and took over 100,000 feet of lumber to construct.

61

While building and logging were the focus of much attention in the valley, mining was still an economic factor. In early 1914, the *Methow Valley Journal* reported that:

• *"W.V. Looney and Dennis Overturf take the contract to do assessment work at the mines on Goat Creek."*

• *"The contract to carry the mail to Slate Creek and Barron has been let to Harry Mayfield."*

• *"The Montana Mining Co., who has several good claims on Goat Creek, unloaded a carload of mining machinery Wed. & Thur. Wm. Voight and Wm. Looney superintended the unloading in Pateros."*

• *"A narrow gauge wagon road is being built up Goat Creek to haul a small stamp mill to test ore at the mines there."*

In November, 1915, the new community hall at Rockview was finally finished and a large crowd attended its dedication, marked by a performance at the hall by students and faculty from the Mt. McKinney and Mazama schools.

"Professor Dow opened the program with a fitting address complimenting the public spirit of the community in constructing the magnificent building. A sumptuous supper, games, and a get together meeting comprised the evening's entertainment."

The next week, a large crowd assembled again, this time for a Basket Social and Dance. Some $22 resulted from the sale of baskets which went towards paying for the Hall.

The Montana Mine up Goat Creek closed for the winter the week of November 10, 1915. It was a good time to close because that winter started at Mazama with a bang. By the first of December, there was three feet of snow on the level. Will Looney's new barn collapsed from the weight of the snow.

But the spring of 1916 came early and water began to make its appearance in the river the first week of March. This was good news because it meant that some of the wells that had gone dry for winter would again have water. In preparation for the high waters of spring, a suspension bridge was put in at Mazama and a cable bridge with a cage was put across the Methow below the Weeman Bridge.

By May, spring activities were in full swing. The Mazama baseball team had a dance and *"cafeteria supper"* at the Rockview Hall to raise money. Baseball practice was held on the local diamond,

This cable bridge near the present Weeman Bridge served the Mt. McKinney area.

east of current Mazama Bridge. The May 4, 1916, issue of the *Journal* reported that *"the first auto of the season reached Mazama with Reuben Hotchkiss at the helm."*

———————

When World War I came, young men in the Methow registered for conscription draft into the United States Forces. In June of 1917, a Home Guard regiment was formed for North Central Washington, headquartered in Wenatchee, and had as its goal the registration of 1,000 men from various locations. In the Methow precincts, Mazama registered 11 men, Winthrop 76, Twisp 73, and Carlton 15.

The Methow had its own battalion. Non-commissioned officers would meet one night per week in addition to conducting regular drill on Tuesday nights. In July of 1917, it was announced that Okanogan would be required to furnish 143 men and 42 would come from the Methow. By lottery, Mazama residents Dennis Overturf and William F. Voigt were chosen, but were not among those to be sent off the following month. By the time the war was over, the Methow war dead included some of the Methow's finest young men. Years later a monument would be erected in the cemetery in their honor. These brave men were: Joseph E. Blatt, Carl F. Boesel, Thomas J. Pruitt, and Reuben O. Hotchkiss.

By the time of World War I, telephones were in use throughout the valley, except in Mazama, but in some cases up to twenty-two families would be on the same line. During the war, the telephone operator had a special ring combination which meant for everybody to pick up the receiver and listen to a big news event about the war.

———————

The year of 1917 brought developments to the educational facilities in the area. On HES 84, just west of the Mazama Bridge (92), Lou Arnold had built a log cabin. He moved to new quarters in about 1917, thus making his cabin in Mazama available for use as a one-room school. Before the school was located in Lou Arnold's cabin, it had been situated on the

An early Mazama school was in a log house on the Fulton place (HES 84). The house had been built by Mr. Arnold, who was said to have been a retired Texas Ranger. Mr. Arnold moved to a new home and let the community use the old house for a school (62a). This class, probably the class of 1917 or 1918, is, left to right: Arnold Parkinson, Keith Patterson, Hewlet, Ray Patterson, Ella Wehmeyer, Nadine Holloway, Carol Patterson, Opel Peters, teacher, and Hazel Patterson.

other side of the river near the McLeod Hotel, where the ditch crossed the road. The school was located in Lou Arnold's cabin for only a few years. A new school was built in 1921 on the other side of the river, and became the school's permanent location. Presently, the building is the Mazama Community Club building.

———————

In the August 3, 1917, edition of the *Methow Valley News,* a small news item appeared which in a way marked the end of an era:

> *"Mr. and Mrs. Guy Waring were passengers out yesterday for the Atlantic coast where they will remain indefinitely. Rbt. Greene succeeds to the management of the business at Winthrop."*

Although sometimes controversial, there is no question that Guy Waring was a most influential pioneer in the Methow Valley and, in fact, in all of Okanogan County. He was involved in nearly every aspect of the community and its economy. He had been a cattleman, merchant, orchardist, and public official, and owned everything from a saloon to a sawmill. His enthusiasm affected the growth and attitude of the whole community. His departure was definitely newsworthy.

The Holloways and the Looneys
(Excerpts from Ethel Holloway's diary)

———————

About the time John McKinney left the area, growth in the Mazama area was brisk. Claims were being filed, timber cut, farms planted, houses built, and dreams turned into reality. The dreams of the Holloways and the Looneys from Spokane would have a significant impact on the community of Mazama. The following account of the two families is taken in large part from Ethel Holloway's memoirs.

Lester Holloway, the son of a Nebraska homesteader, and Ethel Callahan, the daughter of a Minnesota school teacher and mining enthusiast, met in school in Spokane. Ethel's father, Sylvester (Ves) Callahan, had taken the family, including Ethel, her brother, and her sister, Olive, on a trip during the summer of 1904. They went up to Canada, down to Oroville, and up the Methow across Early Winters Creek.

Ves Callahan had learned of a mine on Cooper Mountain at Mazama. He had always been interested in mines, so four years later, when his daughter, Ethel, had married Lester Holloway and his daughter, Olive, had married Will Looney, Ves made both of his sons-in-law a deal: He would give each of them $150 to go to the Methow and work for the summer on a prospect mine located on Copper Mountain. Lester and Will bought a team and a hack, and along with equipment from their homes, headed for Mazama with the idea of spending a summer in the beautiful Methow Valley.

It was June, 1910, when the two men reached the swollen Columbia River at Brewster and found that the cable on the ferry boat was out. The boat coming up the river would catch the cable but would lose it near the top. Finally, after the men waited three days, the boat made its trip up the river and managed to hold the cable. Lester and Will were the first wagon on the ferry and had a frightening trip over the roaring, muddy Columbia. By noon, they were among trees on a mountain road traveled by freighters, up into the Methow Valley. They stopped the first night at Gamble Mill and the second at Joe Lydas's place, and then went down Benson Creek, into the Methow, and to the town of Twisp.

Lester, Will, and party proceeded up the south side of the Methow past the Thompson place, over Wolf Creek, and up a rough steep hill into heavy timber country. Whoever was driving at the time wasn't paying attention and the wagon ran into a tree. The collision broke the wagon tongue, so Lester and Will camped right on the spot until they made a new tongue for the hack. The next day they drove on and reached Copper Mountain (Sandy Butte) and found the spot Ves Callahan had described.

Lester and Will were struck by the beauty of the surroundings — tall mountains, beautiful yellow trunk pines, and the impressive carved bluff called Goat Wall. They were in thick pine grass above their knees and so jubilant in their surroundings that they hopped off the hack and rolled in the lush grass. They turned the horses loose and the first thing the horses did was to treat themselves to a good roll in the grass, too. The next morning, Lester and Will packed the horses and went up the mountain along the creek and easily found the mine. Since the mine was near the creek on a level place, it was a good camp-

ing spot and they stayed there while they did their promised assessment work.

By the time the prospecting work was finished, both the Holloway and Looney families had made up their minds to locate in the valley rather than return to Spokane. Lester filed on a piece of land just at the foot of McKinney Mountain which had recently been opened for homesteading.

An old house and well sat about four miles down the valley from their campsite at Copper Mountain, and in the yard of the house was a sign which read "Meals 25¢ - 35¢ for a gouge." Will bought a relinquishment from Roma and Pauline Johnson just at the foot of Copper Mountain (Sandy Butte) where a creek (later named Looney Creek) emptied. He found a cabin by the creek and moved his family in.

The Marvin Perrines lived next to the Holloways in a little log cabin at the foot of the Lucky Jim Mine. Marvin was working the mine and gave Lester a month or so of work. It was a tough job for Lester. It was so cold that when the men would come down for dinner, icicles were

Holloway homestead in Mt. McKinney (26).

hanging off their clothes. The men would strip, put on dry clothes, and return after lunch to face the tunnel and the water coming from the rocks at every angle. The workers took items such as an old sewing machine or other items for pay, and somehow managed to survive the winter.

Will Looney's sister, Minnie, married Fred Patterson in Cheney and had heard of the beauty of Mazama. The Pattersons were excited about pioneer life and decided to join the Looneys. They filed a claim next to the Looneys on the river (HES 82). Fred Patterson cleaned up the land and started farming, and the farm remained in the family for several generations. Larry Patterson, Fred's grandson, still kept a few cows on the place in the 1990s.

Transportation and the early roads were quite a problem for the settlers in the upper Methow Valley. Obviously, crossing the river was an obstacle. When the water was low, the Methow River could be crossed at the Perrine Ford, about a mile downriver from the present Weeman Bridge, and the well-traveled road to town could be used. Later, there were two ways to cross the river to get mail and visit. One was a narrow cable bridge across at Mazama. Olive Looney got used to walking this shaky bridge and had fun shaking it to scare her friends.

The second way across the river was by a cage cable bridge located across from the McKinney Mountain area, near the Perrine ford. One would step in a little cage and pull oneself across by the cable. Next, in about 1913, the Weeman Bridge (named after the Weeman family who lived adjacent to it) was built. The Holloways and the Weemans became close friends and Lester Holloway was put in charge of building the approach to the bridge. This was the first job for Les that paid real money.

Lester was involved in other activities which benefited the entire community. For instance, homesteaders had made a small ditch which served a bit of the McKinney Mountain area. It wasn't satisfactory, so Lester got together with the Morrows, who lived just below him, and built a larger ditch system. They went about a mile and a half above the Weeman Bridge and got all the homesteaders who lived in between to help in the construction. They surveyed the entire ditch with a level and a straight edge.

Despite all of Lester's activities, the Holloways were far from financially secure. They needed to raise more money if they were going to do more than merely exist. Their parents had helped them out a little from time to time, but this was not a long-term solution. So, Ethel Holloway decided to teach at the Mt. McKinney school. She earned $75 a month which enabled Lester to hire some help. During the winters, Lester Holloway would ride a horse through the snow dragging a log to make a trail to the schoolhouse for Ethel and the students. He made a short cut through the woods and across the field. Ethel would ride her horse to school, "but turn her back towards home." (A trained horse would return home if directed.)

The second year Ethel taught, Lester was able to buy five little Jersey heifers. This was the start of their dairy

Ethel Holloway's photograph of the first Mazama bridge. The bridge was located approximately where the present bridge is located.

farmers killed many rattlesnakes and cemented their dens so they could not get out. During one snake roundup, 135 rattlers were killed as they came out of a den.

Ethel, along with the rest of the community, was also pleased with the arrival of telephones and electricity in 1915. Ethel recalls, *"what a joy that was."* Of course, the phone was a party line and all the settlers joined in visiting with one another. Ethel remembers that Mrs. Wehmeyer and Mrs. Carrol always

herd. Considering Ethel was a city girl from Spokane, she adapted well to the role of farmer's wife. At one point she hand-milked ten cows while Lester milked sixteen. Her milking career came to an abrupt end when a notorious kicker stepped very close behind her. She asked Lester to move it away. Lester assured her that the cow wouldn't kick her and to stand up and move out. Well, she stood up and, sure enough, the cow kicked her. Ethel set down her pail and said to Lester *"I hope you enjoy milking my ten cows along with your sixteen,"* and she never milked again.

One of the things Ethel liked about living in the McKinney Mountain area was the small number of snakes on that side of the river. She had seen a bull snake but never a rattlesnake. On the other side of the river where her friends the Weemans lived, rattlesnakes were numerous. The

Lester and Ethel Holloway with their daughter, Nadine, in about 1912.

said good night over the party line before they went to bed. Next came the arrival of electricity. Telephones and lights in the houses and barns were great benefits and a joy to Mazama residents. The arrival of each was a major event and savored by the whole community.

Ethel was in a good position to compare locations in the Mazama area. Lester bought and sold many pieces of land over the early years. He bought a timber claim across the road from their McKinney Mountain home, along with HES 250, the place at Early Winters which was later owned by Jack and Elsie Wilson. Lester and Ethel owned the Gunn ranch high above the present Big Valley Ranch for a number of years, the old Wehmeyer home in Rockview, old man Briggs' place above them, and a piece of land next to the Weeman place. They paid for improvements to their property with income from the resales and from the sale of logs to Ballard's Rockview Mill, the Fender Mill, and the Gambel Mill.

Lester was forced to sell the ranch when he became very ill and underwent an operation in Pateros, and was no longer able to do the hard work necessary to keep the ranch running. The Holloways moved out of the valley for a while, but eventually returned and rented a house in Winthrop. As times got tough, Lester returned to ranch life and Ethel stayed in town. Lester's brother, Wesley, came to the valley with his family and lived on the ranch with Lester. Eventually, Lester acquired the Frank Lang place, just above Lester's ranch, for Wesley and his family. Wesley moved out when Ethel moved back to the ranch for the summer. Lester

bought a herd of goats to eat most of the brush off the new field, and then had Mr. Coffin from Twisp shoot out the stumps. Lester sold the goats and it wasn't long until he had yet another field of alfalfa.

In 1936, Lester rented his fields to the Northern Seed Company to raise seed. The arrangement did not work because Lester's fields were apparently not good places to raise seed. The company went broke after two years, and Lester was its receiver.

Lester had been urged to run for County Commissioner. He ran as a Democrat, but received much help from his fine friends, George Zahn and Leroy Wright, who took him on their Republican caravan through the county. When Lester was elected, he and Ethel moved to Winthrop. While Lester was Commissioner, the county got out of debt and built a much-needed addition to the court house. He was a conscientious and popular Commissioner and ran for a second term. During his 12 years as Commissioner, Lester and Ethel sold the ranch and used much of their savings, but felt good about doing a public good.

The Otto Bernbeck family bought the Holloways' place in 1946. The Bernbecks had been living in Twisp since 1931 and were well acquainted with Les, who sold it to them with no down payment. Otto raised potatoes and pigs and built a 120-foot log potato cellar on the property. Other than the new cellar, the place stayed about the same until 1950 when Bernbeck traded it for a place in Snohomish and moved away.

To complete the Holloway story, it is important to note that on August 22, 1972, Lester and Ethel celebrated their 64th wedding anniversary, each at the age of 85. In September of that same year, the opening of the North Cascades Highway was a celebration Lester had worked a lifetime to witness. Lester was chosen to cut the ribbon to start the caravan of cars over the highway, and he rode with Governor Evans. It was greatly satisfying for Lester and Ethel to participate in this event and see the plaque on the side of the road with Lester's name included along with Jack Abrams, Morris Bolinger, Leonard Therriault, and of course George Zahn, who did so much to make the highway a reality.

Angus McLeod

In 1918, Angus McLeod home-steaded HES 113, an 114-acre piece about a half mile east (down valley) of the Mazama Bridge. Angus was born in Glengary, Canada, and came to the Okanogan Valley in the early 1890s to seek his fortune in the mines. He was a skilled workman and furniture maker, and built his home in the pines of Mazama where he lived for 29 years. Angus built a commercial building which housed a store, the post office, and accommodations for room and board. Angus was postmaster at the facility for 12 years until his death in 1928.

Next to the bridge at Mazama, Angus had a spot on the river which was just right for picnics. He allowed the area to be used as a community gathering area, complete with an outdoor dance floor. Down the road was a good-sized clearing that became the official Mazama baseball field and hosted contests between the Mazama home team and Winthrop, Robinson, Rockview, and even Twisp.

The Angus McLeod Building in Mazama served as a hotel, saloon, store, post office, and community gathering place for many years. The only identification found with this picture was "Dad Callahan 3rd." This could have been Lester Holloway's and Bill Looney's father-in-law.

The Welch Family

The Welch family story is related at this point, not because of any special events, but because it is typical of that of the early settlers in the Mazama area. Gordon Welch was one of four children who moved with the family to their home-stead at the age of one. He recalled the following memories of his early life in the Early Winters area.

As was the case with many who ended up on the Pacific Coast, Gordon's father, Alva Welch, farmed in Iowa before he got involved in the building trade in north Seattle. In 1912, Gordon was born, and the following year Alva moved the family to Mazama and built a house above Early Winters Creek on HES 91 (later part of the Shafer ranch and presently referred to as the "Rattlesnake House"). Alva was a craftsman and the house he built had special features such as siding, overhanging windows, and detailed wood work, features most other homes lacked. Most of the economy of Mazama was on the barter system, so Alva got the promise of service instead of cash in return for his work. Because of his craft and talent, his services

The Welch house, presently known as the "Rattlesnake House" (97).

were in considerable demand by neighbors.

The original road ran right in front of the Welches' house on the north side, the barn was to the west. Across the road and down the bank about 100 feet were a spring and shallow well. All the water for the house was hauled from here and the spring water kept the milk cool. The Welches had twelve to fourteen cows, fed the milk to the pigs, and sold the cream once a week to get a few dollars for spending money. They could sell their cream in two places in Winthrop - at the cheese maker's down by the bridge or at the Okanogan Creamery.

The creamery used the feed store next to the bank as a pickup point. If cheese sales were not very good, the cheese maker didn't buy the cream, and sometimes the feed store didn't take it either. When this happened, the Welches had to take the cream all the way to Twisp to sell. Between logging, building, and the dozen cows, Alva managed to make a living.

The years passed and Gordon started school. It was a long walk to Goat Wall where the one-room log school was located for a few years. In mid-winter, Gordon walked through the snow which packed down hard on the trail and froze firm in the zero-degree temperatures. By late winter and spring, temperatures rose a bit by afternoon, and by the time the children began their walk home from school, the snow had begun to melt. This made for an awful struggle for Gordon and his young friends as their short little legs broke through the snow crust. By this time of year, Gordon couldn't wait for the snow to be gone.

The school at Goat Wall existed for only a few years. A larger, more permanent school was built by the bridge across the river from Patterson's place on a piece of ground owned by Ed Kagle, HES 114 (now the community building). The move shortened Gordon's daily trip a bit and allowed him more time to help out at home. The move probably also made for more regular school attendance.

A primary source of cash for early upper valley farmers was selling cream. Besides articles in the Journal telling of the demand for cream, this advertisement appeared regularly.

Gordon recalled the Indians at Early Winters when he was a child. Between 100 and 150 Indians would come to Mazama in late summer. They came on horses with their entire families, carrying their possessions in big woven baskets. They made camp at the confluence of Early Winters Creek and the Methow River in the area which became part of the Early Winters Campground. The Indians carried beautiful tapered three-prong spears to catch salmon. The men caught fish, and the women and children walked up Early Winters Creek and picked berries. The men built large racks out of logs and smoked the fish, and the women mixed their berries with the fish to make a paste called pemmican.

The big mine boom was generally over by the teens, but a number of small mines were still working and individual prospectors were plentiful. The Welch family became acquainted with one old-timer who came through the area regularly every year. He was a typical prospector, complete with a pick and shovel, a donkey, a dog, and a .38 revolver on his hip. He would stop and visit the Welches and then move on, but would never tell where he was digging. Apparently, he would mine each summer and make enough money from his efforts to live well for the rest of the year in Seattle.

One year after the prospector left Alva's house, Alva noticed two men on horseback following the old fellow. The miner didn't go too far that evening as he had spent a lot of time visiting the Welsh family, and made camp a little early. He built a fire and settled down for the night, but long before the other two men were aware of it, the old miner had vanished, giving them the slip.

The miner stopped by the Welches a few more times on his way into the mountains in the spring. He would come out in the fall and always stayed at the Winthrop Hotel. On one such stop he didn't come down for breakfast. The manager eventually went up to his room and found him dead in bed with his sack of gold nuggets under his pillow.

By 1934, the Welsh family found that life was just too tough in Mazama and decided to leave and make some money elsewhere, and eventually return to the area. Charlie Woods agreed to look after their place and care for the stock in exchange for being allowed to cut and keep the hay. That winter, a couple of big storms hit. One night, four feet of snow fell on top of what already was there and the barn roof collapsed and broke the back of the saddle horse. Charlie let the team go. They ran down the valley and, unattended, starved to death. The harnesses and equipment rusted and were ruined, and the Welch family never returned to Mazama.

The Overturf Family

A little less than a mile up the trail from the Welch place, past HES 92, Dennis Overturf, from the Wenatchee area, had staked a claim, HES 93. By 1914, he had completed enough of the house so Dennis, his wife, Ellen, and their newborn son, Vernon, could move in. Dennis had staked the homestead at Mazama and worked on the house while the family lived in Twisp. The road went along the bank behind the house, around the barn that sat on a little flat, and then on up valley to HES 94. There was a path down by the fruit cellar, behind the little separator house.

The family raised some hay and Dennis built a ditch from the Methow River which extended well over a mile up the river to supply water for both HES 93 and 92. Building a ditch to the proper grade through rocky soil and moving huge boulders by hand and a one-horse scraper was hard work. Dennis used great quantities of blasting powder and eventually got the job done. Dennis, a hard worker, also sold some timber to the Fender Mill, but spent a lot of time cutting cedar on Early

Winter Creek to make fence posts. He would haul these to Winthrop and sell them for 15¢ each.

Life on the homestead was rough for the family, particularly during the cold winters. In fact, the snow was so deep when Dennis's daughter, Merle, was born in February, 1917, that she had to be delivered by Dennis and a neighbor, Mrs. Welch, because the doctor was unable to make it to the house.

When Vernon was old enough to go to school, he had to ford either the Methow River or Early Winters Creek. He usually crossed the Methow and went to the Mazama School along the road under the Goat Wall. He generally rode his horse, but in winter it was very difficult for Vernon and his sister to get to school. The neighbors had built the small one-room Goat Wall School on HES 94 for the few families that lived in the area, but when the larger school by the bridge was built the

The Overturf homestead house in a typical Mazama winter. The house and farm were later purchased by the Short family and occupied by their daughter and son-in-law, Harold Grant, until the Shafers purchased the property in 1945 (99).

"neighborhood" school was not used. So, the Overturfs moved down valley for the winter.

During several winters, the Overturfs moved into the building in Mazama that housed a store and the post office. The post office was on the right side of the building, and the store was on the left. Upstairs, there were a number of rooms along with quarters for the proprietor. The Overturfs kept their cows out back near the milking barn. Vernon's mother would cook for the boarders who were mostly bachelor miners working in various small mines and claims in the Mazama area. The Overturfs also lived in this building after it had been moved to the McCloud place, a half mile down river from the Mazama Bridge. One winter, they lived in Winthrop in the back of the feed store next to Shafer's grocery store, now called the Emporium.

The best arrangement, however, was when they wintered at the Cooper place in Rockview. This was a good farm with lots of land and a good place to keep the Overturfs' cows. George Cooper had a business out of the valley, so leasing the farm to Dennis was quite convenient. Cooper visited the farm frequently and always remained interested in the place. When Dennis died in the late summer of 1929, a good friend of Dennis and George Cooper, Carl Weller, stepped in to help run the farm. Carl was a logger who had been helping with the milking on the farm prior to Dennis's death.

Bad luck continued for the rest of the Overturfs after Dennis's death and also for the Coopers. One weekend, when George Cooper and his son were visiting the farm, they and Carl Weller decided to set out a group of apple trees. They came up with the idea that instead of digging holes to plant the trees, they would use dynamite to create the holes. They set a number of charges, lit the fuse, and went inside to have lunch. They counted the charges as they went off, and by the time lunch was over, all but one of the charges had blown. When Carl went to investigate, the remaining charge blew up and killed him.

After this, Vernon's mother had to sell the cows. With both Dennis and Carl gone, the family could no longer manage the farm tasks. They moved into the Holcomb house in town, just across the bridge from the school. At the time, Vernon was in the eighth grade, a man in many ways, but still unable to make a living to support his family. His mother took in a couple of teachers as boarders, but this didn't result in much of an income. In a few years, their debts were too great. The family could no longer pay the taxes on the ranch at Mazama, and lost it in a tax sale. The farm was purchased by their neighbors and was eventually occupied by Edith Short.

The Wehmeyer Family

In search of his fortune and future, William H. (Bill) Wehmeyer left Pasco, Washington, in 1892 and struck out for the Methow Valley to find a homestead. He found the spot he was looking for six miles northwest of Winthrop at what would come to be known as Rockview. Bill cut

Bill Wehmeyer built this house at the turn of the century. It was later occupied by his son, Jack, and in 1996, the house was completely renovated and modernized (15).

and Jack took over his father's homestead farm.

Bill's brother, Fred Wehmeyer, claimed HES 180, a 34-acre parcel east of the Weeman Bridge. Bill's brother-in-law, H.H. (Hank) Johnson, took a homestead next to the claim of Bill's son, Charlie. Around 1900, Hank and Bill set up a sawmill by the road just below the house. This led to the Wehmeyers' domination of the Rockview community. The mill probably supplied the Methow Trading Co. with the lumber it sold.

After growing up in Rockview, William's son Harley Wehmeyer, moved up the valley to Mazama where he established his own

trees, cleared land, and built a cabin. By 1894, he had talked his wife, Ella, into joining him on the homestead. Ella rode for seven days in a four-horse rig with a baby on her lap to her new home. Her brother-in-law, Fred, drove the wagon through Coulee City, ferried the Columbia, then traveled to Silver down Texas Creek, which was mostly washed out in the floods of that year.

The Wehmeyer family would grow to play a major role in the growth and future of the upper Methow and Mazama area. William and Ella had 5 sons: Ray died as a young man, Harley settled HES 81, Lou built on lower part of HES 81, Charlie settled a homestead west of his father,

In front of the house, Wehmeyer built a fine barn that stood until the winter of 1995. The structure had appealed to a passing tourist in the 1980s who had it listed as a historical building, thus requiring the new highway to be built so as to avoid its destruction. But, the snow of 1995 took it down(15).

homestead in 1909. After clearing a few acres and building a shack, Harley found a bride, Bertha Vidger from Atholl, Idaho, who had come to Rockview to visit her sister and brother-in-law. Bertha's sister was running the cook shack at the Rockview Mill and her brother-in-law was working at the mill. Bertha stayed to help her and met Harley in 1910. They married the same year. Although they moved into Harley's shack, they started at once to build a new house which would be their home in Mazama for 54 years. Harley worked at clearing the land to raise hay for his horses and about thirty head of dairy cows.

Harley particularly liked horses and was a packer of some note. He packed for Hazard Ballard when Hazard had a packing business at Lost River, and for the U.S. Forest Service. Harley was head packer for the 1933 North Cross State Highway survey team. With the packing went the work of building many of the trails throughout the back country. The Pasayten Wilderness was part of Harley's world and was as familiar to him as the trails and hills between Winthrop and Mazama where he grew up.

Lou Wehmeyer had filed on a homestead across the present road from Harley, next to the river. It was reported that Lou didn't prove up on the land, so Fred Patterson filed on the place and got it. After this, Lou and Fred were bitter enemies for life. Later, however, Lou got forty acres from his brother, Harley, and built the house and barn which still stand in the 1990s.

Harley Wehmeyer's house in Mazama in 1990. (59)

Chapter 4

The 1920s - Logging, Daily Service, and New Arrivals

Exciting and noteworthy events occurred in the area during the 1920s and were recorded in the *Methow Valley Journal*. On July 24, 1924, the *Journal* began its twelfth year of publication with the headline: "TWISP BURNED LAST NIGHT." In the same issue, the paper recalled that the past *"two most important events in Winthrop's rapidly growing prosperity"* were first, the installation of the electric light and power plant, and second, the incorporation of the Town of Winthrop.

A note in the August 14, 1924, edition of the paper reported that *"E.H.C. Ramm is doing carpenter work to enlarge the Winthrop Hospital to accommodate 2 more beds,"* and later noted that *"the Winthrop Hospital is being equipped with a complete set of plumbing."* The same summer, Elbert Cassal started promoting his Winthrop - Mazama Stage which ran Mondays, Wednesdays, and Fridays by "Auto Speed Truck." The timbers were replaced on the Goat Creek bridge and the Mazama bridge was "tightened," which was undoubtedly comforting for Elbert on his "Auto Speed Truck" trips.

Logging was prospering in Mazama. The Rockview Mill had closed, but the Goat Wall Mill owned by Peters & Sons and the Fender Mill near the Weeman Bridge were in operation. During one spring drive at the Fender Mill, it was reported that *"A million feet of logs were moving toward the mill where booms are ready to divert them into the mill pond. The drive lasts for days and there is much interest in the valley in the drive's success."* A steady stream of cars made the loop between the Weeman Bridge and Mazama to see the floating logs.

In addition to the log drives, the Methow was the scene of large sheep drives in the 1920s and 1930s. Sheep gave way to cattle in later years, but in the early 1920s sheep were big business. Sheep grazing was generally done by stockmen outside the valley, while the cattle people were local. The sheep grazed from the Columbia River to the Canadian border, following the mountain ridges on both sides of the valley. The drive routes went right up along the crests and ridges, down the river drainage, and up the other side to the back country valleys.

The drives lasted all summer. Grazing sheep through this beautiful country might sound like an ideal summer outing, but in reality it was a tough and rugged way to make a living. Constant supervision was needed, and even then the losses were often significant. A 1921 Forest Service report estimated the following losses among 11 sheep outfits:

150 lost to poison (plants)
60 killed by wolves or coyote
35 killed by bear
500 strayed

While these losses were out of nearly 30,000 sheep, the numbers were nonetheless considered high.

IST

tje Building
, WASH.

Kenison
DIRECTOR
mbalmer
sp   Pateros.

Model 789
Price $9.50

ssards
r what
re most
setry

freedom, com-
:. **Model 382**
rtable elastic
dium length
cut straight
icately boned.

tout figure is
der bust with
:k; a circular
: assures com-

low as $2.00

shop

sists of an Ointment which Quickly
Relieves by local application, and the
Internal Medicine, a Tonic, which assists
in improving the General Health.
Sold by druggists for over 40 Years.
F. J. Cheney & Co., Toledo, Ohio.

FOR SALE—5 head of horses.
These will go at your own price.
Some big bargains.
                    B. G. EDSON.

A. L. FOX
Auctioneer
Farm Sales.
Livestock.
Satisfaction Guaranteed
Phone 142 for dates
OKANOGAN   -   WASH.

My Home For Sale
Price is right. See Thos. J.
Prewitt, or write me at Soap
Lake.   F. D. DeLANCEY.

METHOW LODGE No. 126
K. of P.
Meet at their Castle
Hall every Wednesday
Evening. All Visiting
Brothers are invited.
R. M. BADGER, C. C.
STANLEY NICKELL, K. R. & S.

MT. GARDNER LODGE
No. 237, I. O. O. F.
Meets every Tuesday
Evening in their hall at
Winthrop.
Visiting Brothers are cordially invited
Officers—Roy M. Paul, N. G.; Wm.
H. Vaughan, V.G.; E. A. Allison, Sec.;
G. A. Moore, Treas.

way, 2 miles from Winthrop.
Price $7,000 if sold at once. One-
third down; easy terms on balance   W. C. HANKS,
                    Winthrop, Wash.

Tutt's Pills
Induce regular habit, good
digestion.   Relieve the
dyspeptic and debilitated
and tone up the system
AGAINST MALARIA

MT. McKINNEY REBEKAH LODGE 203
Meets every 1st and
3rd Thursday even-
ings in each month
in Fraternal Hall,
Winthrop. Visiting
members are always
made welcome.
Officers—Pricie Vaughan, N. G.;
Auburn Tyler, V. G.; Mary E. Albin,
R. S.; Alfred Tyler, F. S.; Simon
Veazey, Treas.

BARBER
SHOP

SHEARS SHARPENED.
BRING THEM IN.
WORK GUARANTEED

G. A. MOORE
Winthrop

Winthrop---Mazama Stage

ELBERT CASSAL, Proprietor

Phone No. 3w5.

CARRY PASSENGERS, FREIGHT, PACKAGES AND MAIL
ON REGULAR STAGE DAYS—MONDAYS, WED-
NESDAYS AND FRIDAYS BY AUTO
SPEED TRUCK.
SPECIAL TRIPS AT ANY TIME.
LET ME HAUL YOUR WOOD.

gan dispersing afte
able evening to l
by all.
    A dark shadow
the little group of
they gathered aro
ed leader after the
parted to listen fo
to those kind, fa
uplifting words of
struction.   There
tempt at cheerful
attentive listeners
encouragement to
soon departing S
within the depths
boys was a forb
lessness and a ne
failure in their r
tempt to maintai
troop in Winthro
aid of Mr. Hearne
    Mr. Hearne w
and leave what h
unfinished work
Methow Valley,
and he departed
ing a warm place
the   Winthrop I
wish him much su
ness wherever he
    Plans are bein
finish the work
Forward, Boys!
support of the co
not afford to fai
start.   Let's Go!
                VESTER

PETERSE
Mrs. Selna Su
Illinois, and Pete
Winthrop, were
day morning by
peace John E. P
vester and E. L
natchee served a
ceremony.—Wen

WAR
Persons drivi
quested to clo
driving through
Anyone violatin
cuted by law.
                B. C

WEATHER
                Temper
                Max. M
Aug. 24....87
Aug. 25....87
Aug. 26....96
Aug. 27....94
Aug. 28....86
Aug. 29....76
Aug. 30....72

An August, 1924, edition of the Journal carried an advertisement for Elbert Cassal's new "Auto Speed Truck" service to Mazama along with other typical advertisements and news items of the day.

he left his bear hounds at Billy Robinson's place at Lost River and headed into town.

In Winthrop, Peterson got word of the grizzly having scattered 150 sheep in Lost River country. This news made possible a new plan of attack. He would not go directly there, but rather would strike farther north, through Windy Pass. If that plan failed, he and his party would then head for Granite Mountain country, on the theory that the grizzly might follow the sheep in that direction.

A month after the grizzly bear incident, a big cougar made his appearance at the J.A. Cassal ranch. "Government Hunter" Peterson, Roma Johnson, and Ed Ramm took up his trail.

Not all of the news was about the growing economy, however. In early October, 1924 "Government Hunter" Peterson showed up in Winthrop to get resupplied. He reported that he was about a week behind a big stock-killing grizzly bear. He had lost track of it near Falls country, and since he was low on supplies,

But, according to the newspaper, the cougar "made his getaway." In December, the news came that a cougar had killed a fourteen year old boy ten miles west of Okanogan, and in January, a Winthrop man killed a cougar at the head of Bear Creek, eighteen miles from the site of the tragedy.

Fear and feelings ran high. Every week from January until June, the paper carried stories, letters, and editorial material on cougars and cougar killings. In the January 15, 1925, issue of the *Journal's* "Rockview News" section, the following appeared: *"Since the cougar excitement there are more dogs at school than pupils, as each one has from one to four dogs. So Mr. Cougar better hide out."* Interest seemed to reach a peak when the *Journal* office was selling post cards picturing the dead "Boy Killing Cougar."

Social life went on in spite of the cougars and bears. In October, the dance given by the Mt. McKinney school at the Rockview Hall was a great success, raising $107 toward the purchase of an organ for the school.

January and February of 1925 produced some heavy snowfalls. A common practice was for families to meet for Sunday dinner and for the men to plow snow. Will Haas and W.H. Wehmeyer plowed out the road from Winthrop to the mill in Rockview with eight horses. The February 5th issue of the paper said, *"The people of Rockview want to thank Dr. Murdock for the interest he took in helping us 'V' the roads. He hired a man and team, and we sure needed them before we were through."*

The "V" mentioned in the article referred to the tool used to plow the roads. Plowing was done with a wood "V" consisting of two planks, three inches thick, about twenty-four inches wide, and about twenty feet long, with heavy hinges that allowed the "V" to be set at various widths. Roads in Twisp were plowed with a "V" pulled by a 1918 Army truck.

Mazama residents used two or more teams of horses and each resident would pull the "V" by their section of the road.

Another important improvement which was essential in the development of the Slate Creek district was the bridge across Lost River built by the Forest Service and finished in 1928. Before the bridge, it had been necessary to ford Lost River. Sometimes, however, the river was too high to cross safely. Two miles beyond the bridge at Robinson Creek, the Forest Service had established the Methow Camp Resort, intending it to become one of the state's most popular places for campers, fishermen, and tourists, situated only twenty miles from Winthrop, with good road all the way.

The road west of Mazama saw some improvements as well. The road followed along the bank of the river, past the old school, and then ran in front of the future Early Winters Ranger Station. The road continued across Early Winters Creek past the Cassal place and on to the Arnold homestead on McGee Creek.

The 1920s brought more changes to the schools in the area. The school was moved from the Arnolds' log house on HES 84 to a building on HES 114 near the McLeod Hotel. The state Legislature appropriated $360 for an additional log school at Goat Wall on Calloway Cassal's place, HES 94. The appropriation provided a $60 monthly salary for a teacher, and Mildred McDermott was chosen. Mildred was the daughter of Fred McDermott, a well-known man who ran steamboats on the Columbia River. Mildred boarded with Mrs. Short and rode her horse to school each day.

In the spring of 1925, the *Journal* reported, *"owing to Fred Patterson's ill luck [his wife's health problems] the Mazama Grange has decided to set aside Tuesday Ap. 21 to donate a day's work or money to help him out. Anyone wishing to help with team or single handed is invited . . . The ladies will serve dinner at Harley Wehmeyer's."* The event was a big success. Ten teams and seventeen men worked at clearing, plowing, harrowing, and re-seeding. Additionally, $15 was collected.

In 1928, daily mail service started in Mazama and the Star Route between Winthrop and Mazama was extended to include the west side of the river from the Weeman Bridge to Mazama.

Transportation continued to improve in 1928. The *Journal* announced that summer that the third annual Cascade pilgrimage was to take place which would once again call attention to the possibility of a route across the mountains to the west side of the state. Each year an additional stretch of road was graded and paved from the west side. However, no road building was taking place down the east side to

The Mazama Post Office in the 1920s.

Lake Chelan and up Bridge Creek to the Methow.

Methow citizens felt that this was the key to the future of the Valley. If the county and community didn't bring it about, the citizens would have to wait for the State to build down from the other side, and nobody knew how long that would be. There would be a double purpose for this road: to provide a route for the visitor and sightseer and to establish an outlet for the mineral and chemical resources found in this promising territory. This same campaign for a road had been going on since the road was started in 1895, thirty-three years before.

The 1920s also brought some new families to the area. Their stories are both interesting and typical of those arriving during that period.

Bert Boughey

In 1919, Bert Boughey claimed HES 95, 132 acres four miles west of Mazama just above Gate Creek on the road to Robinson. He built a log house and cleared a cedar forest to make room for a garden. As the years went by, the amount of land under cultivation increased very slowly. People shook their heads and said "Boughey is more of a violin player than a farmer." But it was nice having a violin player in the community, so when H.C. Peters purchased the ranch in 1928, folks were sorry to see Bert just disappear. The only news of Bert was an occasional order for Peters, who was putting in a sawmill, or for someone to cut him a piece of spruce which he described minutely as to thickness of tree, grain, etc. Residents were both pleasantly surprised and mildly astonished to behold half of the magazine section of a Seattle Sunday newspaper telling of "Violin maker Bert Boughey who is becoming famous."

Before buying HES 95 from Bert Boughey, the Peters family had a mill near the Mt. McKinney school. A ditch from the river ran to a natural little slough area which made a mill pond. Peters bought a steam engine to power his sawmill, since he planned to do more than just cut cedar posts. The first work for the engine, however, would be to move R.E. Short's house on HES 92 (later the Shafer house) about a quarter mile east of where it originally sat, to a site more convenient to the barn.

The Wickert Family

The Wickert family had a homestead next to HES 202, Mr. Sloane's place. Mr. Wickert was a fine old German craftsman who had built a nice house for his family. (57) He did building throughout the Mazama area for many years and completed such area landmarks as the large barn for the Kumm family in the McKinney Mountain area.

Wickert gave acreage to his daughters, Marie and Frieda. Marie married a fellow named Crawley who built a house on Little Boulder Creek about fifty feet from the present Highway 20, on a site that is now near the front gate of the Devin ranch. Crawley built a root cellar in the bank of an old wash of the creek and raised some chickens. Marie planted a garden and put flowers around the house. A wagon road and a bridge over the creek ran south of the house, toward the mountain. Crawley didn't stay long at the property, however, and the place changed hands several times. Eventually, the property was bought by Mr. Arbuckle, the neighbor to the west.

Arbuckle was one of the first serious farmers in the area. He cleared land, worked up the soil, and put in a 5-acre orchard south of the Crawley house and 50 acres of peas on HES 202. Arbuckle had problems with both crops, problems typical to Mazama residents. The growing season was too short for fruit trees and the deep snow and deer broke down the tender branches of the trees. The peas grew well but the deer discovered them at the flowering stage and again when the pods were ripe. The neighbors from 800 feet away could hear the "pop, pop, pop" of the pea pods as the deer munched away a big part of the crop. Arbuckle was more than a little unhappy with the deer intrusion. He complained to the game warden, George McDaniels. McDaniels didn't have a ready answer, but in a few days he saw Arbuckle and gave him three boxes of shells with the warning, "don't cripple 'em."

Dr. Malzacher owned the place after Arbuckle and either he or Arbuckle decided that they had no use for the Crawley house. The community needed a church and Sunday school building, so the Crawley house was donated to this worthy cause and moved across the creek about a half mile down valley to a site donated for the purpose. The building was painted and kept in good repair by the ministers. It never had water or a sewer, so the children used two outhouses. A big wood stove heated the building either too much or too little, but Sunday school went on.

The other Wickert girl, Frieda, married Tom Davis and later Tim Wilmurth. Frieda had a house, garden, and chicken coop about 300 yards east of Little Boulder Creek. Evidently, Frieda was not the easiest person to get along with. She liked horses and kept some on the property. This greatly irritated Frieda's husband, Tim. They had no pasture so Tim had to buy feed, which they could ill afford. This apparently led to a number of arguments between Frieda and Tim. One argument culminated with Tim's announcement that he was going to kill himself. After announcing this, Tim marched out of the house carrying his

hunting rifle, and went across the snow to the fruit cellar about thirty feet away. The next sound Frieda heard was the discharge of the rifle.

It was Sunday morning and snowing, so she put on her coat and overshoes and went directly to Walt Stout's house across the road. She told Walt she thought that Tim might have killed himself. Walt didn't know what to do, but knew he didn't want to do anything by himself. He went to the nearby church, which was conducting services, and enlisted Bill Stewart to go with him to investigate. Their worst fears were confirmed. Tim had put his rifle in his mouth and pulled the trigger.

Walt and Bill were careful to note that only one set of tracks led to the cellar, and Frieda was even more careful to do so. Bill called the sheriff and the evidence appeared to clear Frieda of any guilt, although some in the area whispered their suspicions that she had done it. She did go to the cellar after the body was removed and carefully wiped and washed all the jars that had been splattered with blood and flesh. This was regarded by a few as a cold and unsympathetic gesture which only confirmed their theory of who actually killed Tim.

The Sloanes and The Stewarts

Nancy Sloane, a widow with seven children and several grandchildren, left Kentucky by rail in 1908 with all the family's belongings. She eventually homesteaded in Mazama on land with nice timber and level ground, situated on a stretch of the river that didn't appear to flood frequently. Nancy's son, Tom, filed a claim, HES 202, which is part of the present Burkhart and Devin ranches. Nancy filed a claim, HES 200, upriver from Tom, which Tom later purchased from her and added to the larger Sloane ranch. Tom's brother, Robert, filed a homestead claim down valley about a mile. Tom and Robert were farmers, loggers, builders, and they each hacked their ranches out of the wilderness.

Martha Sloane was one of Nancy's ten grandchildren. Daughter of Tom, she was born in Kentucky in 1906, and was two years old when Nancy and crew settled in Mazama. Martha grew up with all the trials and joys of frontier living. She walked several miles down valley along a tree-lined road, over a narrow bridge across Little Boulder Creek to the one-room Mt. McKinney school.

Young Martha Sloane looked forward to social events both in Mazama and, on special occasions, in Winthrop. The Fourth of July was a major occasion in the early West and Winthrop celebrated the occasion in typical style with picnics, ball games, and dances. It was at one of these events that Martha met Bill Stewart, her future husband. Actually Martha met two young men on the Fourth of July, and when she received a letter from one of them a few days later she didn't remember which one he was. She was sixteen years old at the time, but by

the time she was eighteen, she had sorted things out and married Bill Stewart.

Bill was five years older than Martha. Born in 1901, he came to the Methow in 1922. Bill and Martha were married in Wenatchee in 1924 and started out keeping house in a building just downriver from the Weeman Bridge. Bill spent three years working for the mill as yardman. Bill was one of twenty-six men, each with his own team, who hauled logs in the winter of 1929. The temperature reached 47 degrees below zero that winter. Bill guessed that the two horses that died working that season had frozen their lungs when breathing hard.

The remains of the Stewart barn and farmstead in 1990.

One interesting observation made by Martha in later years was regarding the growth and foliage on Sandy Butte, the mountain behind her house. As a small girl, she remembered seeing cattle grazing on the sparsely treed side of the hill. Today, the hill is thickly forested with trees that are 60 to 80 years old. Because there were no known fires or previous logging, the area must have undergone a climate change that is responsible for the new forest cover.

In 1927, Bill and Martha obtained forty acres from Martha's father, Tom Sloane. Only three trees had been cut on the entire place, so Bill went to work clearing most of the rest of the land. He sold logs to the mill and bought back lumber to build his house and barn which took about three years to complete. The home became one of the showplaces of Mazama because of Martha's gardening efforts. Bill bought eight dairy cows from Lester Holloway and, like nearly everyone else, went into the dairy business.

Other homesteaders followed the same general practice, raising some cows, sheep, and chickens. Bill remembers that above the Fender Mill on the north side of the river, the Weeman family had a homestead which spanned the river. Weeman had a patch of red clover and a few cows, but he also had a different product than most. Weeman had 100 to 150 black cats and sold the skins for up to $3 apiece to a fur company. The winter the two horses died from the cold at the mill, Weeman dragged the carcasses up to his place and the cats fed on horsemeat most of the winter. Weeman also had a little wagon and would travel around to where people were butchering and collect scraps to feed the cats.

Bill Stewart left the valley in 1927 to mine in Kellogg, Idaho. He returned and logged or trapped every year until 1944. His traps were set in Little Boulder Creek, Fawn Creek, and Ramsey Creek. Trapping started in the creek bottom where Bill would get fifteen to eighteen mink. When the creek froze, the mink left, so he trapped farther up for marten. He would get about the same number. It was a long trip on snow shoes up to the headwaters of Huckleberry Creek, and he would make his last trip for the season during the first part of January.

Bill also worked at clearing the right of way for power lines when electricity finally came to the valley in the 1930s. Electricity was made possible by the REA, the Rural Electric Administration, a federal government program that subsidized electricity to rural areas that could not be served by private power companies. Land for the lines was mostly dedicated by the property owner. Edgar Hotchkiss was Bill's boss. Besides being an electrician, Edgar was a miner in the Mazama area with diggings along Goat Wall and Flagg Mountain. Like nearly everyone in the area he had to have several vocations to get by in Mazama.

Martha's sister, Selma Sloane, married Earl Short, who had farmed HES 92, and they lived on the Overturfs' homestead, HES 93. Martha's youngest brother, Walter, was born in Mazama, and returned after World War II. He and his brother, Tom, bought the Sloane ranch and sold it to Josh Graves in 1956, who in turn sold it to Aaron Burkhart.

This undated 1920s photograph of Winthrop features a number of buildings that no longer exist. The town's largest building in the center of the photo was Waring's Methow Trading Co. which was located on the corner of Bridge Street and Riverside Ave. The next multi-story building down Riverside Ave. was the Nickel & Sons store which burned in about 1925. The MT Co. burned in about 1928. In the distance the three-story Winthrop School, built in 1912, is clearly seen, and stood until it burned in 1961. A number of the houses in this picture have been kept in repair and are still being occupied. The Winthrop Hotel is in the right center of the picture. The porched building on the left was originally a hotel owned by Harry Greene, Waring's stepson, and moved from the area later occupied by the Pool Hall.

Chapter 5

The 1930s - Mining, Road Building and the Log Chute

The Depression Years

While the Great Depression of the 1930s hit hard across the nation, folks in the upper Methow Valley knew it was going on, but generally didn't feel the crunch. Because nearly everyone in the area lived a subsistence existence as a normal way of life, things went on about the same.

Efforts to get the Cascade Pass built were furthered somewhat with the award of contracts to build additional sections of road which would put people to work. Mining interest increased, perhaps because men didn't have anything else to do and had the time to prospect and promote mines. A group of Seattle men and local men announced plans to open the American Flagg Mine on Goat Mountain. It was reported that rich ore had been reached in the Flagg Mine and the owners were planning to put in a reduction mill on part of the McLeod place (HES 113) they had purchased.

In 1931, the post office was located on the Bertrams' property, HES 114. At this time, W.P. Gadeski decided to open a grocery store in Mazama and initially stored his wares in the post office building. The *Journal* reported that *"as soon as a townsite is laid out a store building will be erected."* The store, built in 1936, was the second mercantile venture in Mazama. The first was during the Hart boom in the summer of 1895 when Frank McCain set up a large tent in what became HES 203. For a few months, McCain sold over the counter to miners here and in Slate Creek, but went out of business when the boom subsided.

Determined not to let the Depression get the better of them, the ladies of the South Fork Civic Club met and made arrangements for a "Depression Party" to be held on October 15, 1931, in the Rockview Hall. Invitations were written on wallpaper and a prize was offered for the *"most amusingly dressed guest."* While the ladies planned the party, the men organized a roundup. Bob Morrow, Jack Wehmeyer, and Montray Cassal brought cows down from the Yellow Jacket

1930s traffic at the Mazama corners of Lost River Road and Goat Creek Road.

range. (It was noted that the cows weren't as fat as usual.) Lots of downed timber in Black Pine Basin made the roundup difficult.

———————

Bill Stewart, Earl Short, and Tom Sloane use a Model T Ford to run a buzz saw to cut wood in the fields on HES 92.

One of the tasks that is facilitated by the Early Winters area snowfall is skidding logs. Here, Ray Patterson, with his team and log tongs, is ready for work.

As the community of Mazama went into the winter of 1931, people felt relatively optimistic. The Fender Mill, located by the Weeman Bridge, was building a chute for logs in Boesel Canyon in back of Leonard Harvey's place, and expected to take its season's run of logs from there through the winter. The log chute was an interesting concept which grew from the desire to take advantage of the force of gravity in moving logs. The chute was actually a trench dug in the ground with teams of horses hitched to plows. Where the ditch crossed rock or ravines, it was built from logs.

To make the chute work, it was iced with the water from Boesel Creek with mops and brooms after work when the temperature was freezing and after the men had already worked a 10-hour day. When it snowed, the chute had to be shoveled by hand with a specially shaped tool made by the blacksmith at the mill.

The logs, up to sixteen feet in length, were skidded to the top of the chute with teams. They were fed in by men with peaveys and slid to the bottom in a short period of time, as long as everything worked properly. All too often, however, logs piled up in the chute and jumped the side, sometimes breaking up. Logs with knots were especially difficult to get to the bottom and several men with peaveys were stationed along the chute to keep the logs going.

The logs were decked at the bottom until they could be loaded on sleds and taken to the mill, where they were again decked by the edge of the mill pond, ready for use in the spring when the mill re-opened. The log chute ran for two years but was only marginally successful. Additionally, it was very dangerous. Fortunately, however, only one accident occurred, when Paul Duffy broke his leg while walking up the chute to work at the same time a log was sent prematurely down the chute.

Most of the men who worked on the chute lived in the area on small farms, in the mill bunkhouse, or in tar paper cabins. The mill had a cookhouse operated by Alma Tate who provided meals for 90¢ per day. Later in the year, the price was increased to $1.05, which caused great unrest and rumors of a strike. In the spring of 1932, the log chute was abandoned when the weather turned warm.

Another mill opened in the area. This one, located on HES 83 (William Looney's old place), was operated by H.C. Peters and his son, Ellis. Peters had closed his Goat Wall Mill on HES 95. He and his son turned water from Early Winters Ditch to fill the mill pond. They cut timber off their land and made apple boxes for the Nickel Brothers' packing house in their shake mill and planer mill.

Dances went on throughout the winter of 1931-32, and there emerged a new group of local music makers. Callaway Cassal, H.C. Peters, and Ken Fulton played for the dance at the school in December as well as the parties to usher in 1932.

The new year, however, brought a real sadness to Mazama with the death of William Looney. He was only fifty years old and in apparent good health. On a March day, he was working sheep with Ethel Holloway at the Holloway ranch when he suddenly collapsed as in a faint and was pronounced dead by Dr. Starr from Winthrop. Joshua C. Cassal also died that spring. He was sixty years old and left five sons and two daughters.

The winter of 1934-35 was good for those who liked snow. A record snowfall fell in Mazama during the last week of January, 1935, when fifty-two inches fell in twenty-four hours. Normally, Mazama got considerably more snow than Winthrop, but in this storm Winthrop recorded the same depth, Twisp received 30 inches, and Carlton 18 inches.

More sad news arrived the next year. In April, 1936, the *Methow Valley Journal* reported:

"Guy Waring, founder of Winthrop, died at his home in Hyde Park, near Boston on March 27. He had been in poor health, but died of a stroke. He was born in New York, Jan 1859, son of Col. George Waring, went to College and after he worked with his father in Newport R.I. until 1884. He married and went with his wife and 3 step children to Portland, Oregon. In 1891, after first locating in Loomis, starting a store and acting as an official in the

early county government, he started a new home and store in what would become Winthrop. The store paid his expenses but on March 1, 1893 the whole venture was consumed by fire. But all his bills were paid and he had $728 in the Bank. There was 4 feet of settled snow that winter, the worse since '62 and he had to remain until May to get out. In '97 he returned to Winthrop where a friend had carried on successfully his business. He remained for 27 years in all. In 1906 his wife died after a 10 year illness. In 1897 he incorporated the Methow Trading Co. and was president until 1924 when mortgagees took over control. In 1917 he married the widow of Geo. Burgess (Harvard '93) and after lived in Milton Mass."

The operators of the Fender Mill ran into trouble during the summer of 1936. A receiver had been appointed and a hearing was set for September.

On the bright side of the economy, reconstruction of two and a half miles of road from the state highway at the Peters Mill in Mazama to Early Winters Creek was in progress. A twenty-three man detail from the Gold Creek Civilian Conservation Corps (CCC) stationed at the Early Winters administration site built the sixteen-foot roadbed. Ranchers helped by clearing right-of-way for the new road.

U.S. Forest Service Builds at Early Winters

The Early Winters Ranger Station seemed to evolve over several years. At one point there was a CCC camp on the northwest side of the creek, but this lasted only a few months as the creek, the camp's source of water, went dry. Cabins were built later to house specialty workers engaged in projects of the Works Progress Administration (WPA), a major government employer for federal construction projects during the Depression. As the station work progressed, these cabins were moved to the compound and eventually torn down.

A major part of the Early Winters Ranger Station was constructed in 1937 by the WPA. A number of local men found work on the project as well. Bill Wehmeyer helped dig the basement, Walt Clark and Rowe Strasbough worked on the project, and Ray Patterson served as assistant ranger. George Wright was the Ranger. When completed, the Early Winter Station became the headquarters of the Pasayten District. A newly completed facility in Winthrop was the Headquarters of the Winthrop District.

The Pasayten area was the focus of considerable attention and probably one reason for the need for a separate Ranger District. The Pasayten Airport was enlarged and completed in the summer of 1936. The building of this strip was a major accomplishment. Bulldozers and equipment were taken from Barron over

This major structure was built on top of Driveway Butte as part of the fire lookout system. All materials were taken to this remote site by pack horse over very steep and rugged terrain. Major functions of the U.S Forest Service during the 1920s and 1930s were fire protection and management of grazing. While there were some cattle, the primary grazing was by sheep in the mountain country from the Columbia River to the Canadian border.

unique architectural style and were supposed to blend with their surroundings using rustic walls, fences, and heavy squared timbers. These projects put very fine craftsmen to work who otherwise would have had no work. The project produced an exceptional station which would one day be included in the National Register of Historic Places.

———————

makeshift roads to this remote spot, and removed after the construction was complete. The expansion of the airport was a huge improvement to fire control capabilities in the area.

Early Winters was typical of the CCC's projects built as a Federal response to the Depression. The buildings had a

A symbol of change in Mazama occurred in November of 1937 when a special meeting of the School Board decided not to open the Mazama school for winter due to projected attendance of only six students.

A promise had been made that if there were eleven or twelve students, the school would be furnished. There were eleven school-age children in Mazama, but parents of five of them wanted their children to go to school in Winthrop. Thus,

U.S. Forest Service buildings at Early Winters.

The last Mazama school, built in about 1921, is today the Mazama Community Club building. A porch and a kitchen have been added. The students shown in this picture were members of a Sunday school class that also used the building.

since it was now possible to run buses, it was considered unnecessary to keep a separate school in operation. The state had assured the school it would employ special equipment to keep the road open to Robinson Creek. It was the end of an era.

On a brighter note, by the mid and late 1930s, upper Methow residents had learned to enjoy the cold and snow of winter. Skiing for fun, instead of just for transportation, had been discovered. Ski lifts were built on Forest Service land near Patterson Mountain and a 1,500-foot rope carried skiers up the slope behind the Sunny M Ranch.

There was a special event called "Ski Frolic" scheduled for Lewis Butte in March, 1938. Skiers went to First Creek in the Cub Creek drainage and then had a downhill run of over a mile back down to the Methow. Mr. Kovack, a teacher who was in charge of the event, declared that the snow was excellent and the course was steep and smooth, thus insuring a very fast run. He also scheduled a *"slalom or turn contest"* which he felt "would be interesting for spectators and skiers alike." A Snow Queen was to be chosen from the high school student body. Spectators were told that the entire Frolic could be seen from their cars.

———————

The Fender Mill went broke in 1937 and managed to limp along for a while. Otto Wagner bought it in 1939. At that time, the lumber business looked better down valley. This was clearly not in the best interest of those holding jobs in Mazama. Nonetheless, everything was moved to the Fender Box Mill in Twisp, and during the next two years, a new sawmill was built on the site. This established Twisp as the commercial center of the Valley.

The summer of 1938 was a dry one and the resulting fires were hard on Mazama. In July, Mr. and Mrs. R.E. Short discovered their barn on HES 93 ablaze at 4:15 in the morning. Two loads of hay were in the barn and the fire spread to the separator house and then to the chicken house. All were burned to the ground. A CCC crew was sent to the site to prevent spot fires later. Shortly after noon the same day, flames were spotted from the Driveway Butte lookout at H.C. Peters's residence and the same CCC crew was called upon to fight that fire.

Alva Sharp

A notable character in the 1930s was Alva Sharp, Guy's brother. Alva was an enterprising fellow, active in mining, prospecting, cattle, and house building. One of Alva's best houses was probably the one he built for Bessie Hardy (see page 41). At the time he built this house, Alva's most profitable activity was making moonshine, and the reliable spring above the house provided an important resource for this activity. After all, a good moonshiner needs a reliable source of water.

For a number of years, Alva had been living with Bessie, who was known for making pretty good beer. Between the two of them, they were able to offer sup-

plies to both locals and travelers to the Slate Creek area. Alva spent quite a bit of time in his mines and was not able to be at home to serve his customers. Bessie, however, was usually there and as the word spread that she had more than liquid refreshment to offer, lots of fellows stopped on their way. Bessie and Alva were married for a period in later years and it was said that the wilder days of moonshine and a roll in the hay were gone but certainly not forgotten.

Floyd and Anna Kent

Floyd and Anna Kent stepped off the train in Pateros on March 31, 1928, and started a life that was typical of many who would inhabit the Mazama area during the next half century. The Kents rented an upstairs apartment in Twisp, and Floyd went to work driving a lumber truck for Wetzel & Son. The work was steady until the company shut down in late fall. At that time, road conditions limited the number of working months. Anna made several trips with her husband to see the country. She made trips to the Fender Mill above Winthrop and to various orchards to deliver box material. By winter, the Kents were generally familiar with the valley.

Like many valley people, Floyd and Anna planned to trap during the winter, so they moved up Libby Creek. Floyd went to Okanogan and bought the winter's grub stake for about $50, and they were set for the winter.

The following winter, the Kents left the valley to find work, but returned in the spring. Floyd went back to driving for

Wetzel and hauling logs out of Fawn Creek to the Fender Mill. They lived in one of the cabins at the mill and became acquainted with what they thought was "a new and lovelier part of the valley." They loved the upper valley so when their first

The Kent house in 1996. The little willow tree has grown and the rock chimney was added in 1975, but other than that, it looks about the same as it did when Floyd and Anna left. (51)

daughter was born in 1930, they bought property in the McKinney Mountain area from Lester Holloway. Lester had subdivided a homestead into 20-acre parcels. Floyd, who was a carpenter by trade, built a cozy two-room house on their 20 acres, just across the road from the Mt. McKinney school. The Kents acquired a cow, a pig, and a horse to till the garden, and planted a grain field to feed the chickens.

The Kents loved the area and their friendly neighbors. They enjoyed sleigh rides up and down the road or across the fields to the Joe Fleishmans, the Frank Kumms, the Lester Holloways, or the Bob

Scotts, who had the adjacent 20-acre ranch. Everyone visited more in those days than in later years. Anna recalled a memorable trip one winter's day when the family left home in a covered bobsled and drove all day through Elbow Canyon and up the Twisp River to a relative's place where they spent the night. The next day, the family drove to Carlton, spent the night at Libby Creek with friends, and then started on two days' travel back home again, visiting all along the way and staying with friends.

In the early 1930s, Anna's sister Helen Read, came to visit and ended up being the teacher at the Mt. McKinney school in 1931. She married Bob Morrow who was farming the Hancock homestead and became a member of the Mazama community.

After teaching at Mt. McKinney, Helen taught for a time in Rockview. The Rockview school was bulging with forty students because of the prospering Fender Mill. This was too much for a one-room school and the teacher, Miss Flint, had a breakdown trying to cope with the challenge. Helen relieved her for the remainder of the year.

During the winter of 1934, work was hard to find, and the Kents moved to Grand Coulee so Floyd could work on the dam. By the summer of 1935, they were back in the Methow and enlarging their home. It was this summer that they planted the weeping willow tree from a switch from Frank Kumm, an addition to the place that lived on through the years and became a "trademark" of the site.

It was about this time that the Azurite Mine was in full swing and the ore trucks rumbled down the road headed for Pateros. Floyd worked at the Azurite Mine for a year. It was hard work and in winter the only way in or out was on snow shoes from Ed Kikendall's station at Robinson Creek. Times were still pretty tight in the Methow, but most felt that they came through the Depression better than other areas. There wasn't much money in circulation, but nobody went hungry because everyone was more or less self-sustaining.

With the coming of the 1940s and the threat of war, the Kent family took work in the defense industry. The work took Floyd to Alaska. The family was in and out of the valley for the next ten years. Finally, in 1953, they pulled up stakes and went to Alaska for nine years. Floyd then felt it was time *"to turn Alaska over to the younger generation,"* so the Kents returned to the Methow to live out their senior years.

While Anna and Floyd retired on the Chewuck River, their daughter, Eleanor, who had married Don Drake, kept the family presence in Mazama by moving into the old Weeman homestead. The Weeman place had changed hands, the original house had burned, and Clarence Stout had built a nice home on the same

old original homestead foundation. After buying the place from Stout, Don went to work for Bill Laney and Norm Hamilton building the roads and utilities for the big Edelweiss real estate development.

Mining Continues in Mazama

During the summer of 1931, considerable attention was focused on mining in Mazama with the promotion and opening

METHOW VALLEY JOURNAL JUNE 18, 1931

Danlee of Mazama

The Modern Miracle Story of a

Cow Pasture That Camouflaged GOLD!

Fairy Stories Still Come True

Do you know that the most amazing recent-day gold strike, occurred LAST FALL, in the Methow River Valley, at Mazama, Washington, north of Winthrop? Do you know that a pioneer prospector of the district, Mr. Hotchkiss, wouldn't believe that profitable gold had all been discovered in the 90's, and that his faith in the natural characteristics of the district were rewarded by the discovery of RICH ORE in a dozen outcropping, at the very grass roots of a Mazama cow-pasture? Do you know that he slept on a bed of gold, sat on a chair of gold, and ate off a table of gold....while doing the necessary development work on his claims this spring? Do you know that Mr. Hotchkiss and his associates of the Mazama Pride Group have leased their rich gold claims to the incorporators of the Danlee Mining Company for NINETY-NINE YEARS....on the exceedingly fair and attractive 10% royalty basis....and YOU now have the opportunity to secure outright ownership units in this lease at the LOWEST PRICE THEY WILL EVER BE QUOTED?

A few years ago a story was told of the "acres of diamonds" that lay at the feet of the discoverers of the South African diamond mines....that had also lain at the feet of generations that preceded those discoverers. TODAY A MODERN INSTANCE of "acres of gold" is being enacted RIGHT IN THIS DISTRICT! Gold....discovered in this area by the old prospectors and abandoned for other fields in '95....again quickens the red-blooded folks of this district into action! And remember: Mazama is a field that requires no back-breaking blazing to it; an automobile road through a fertile valley adjoins the Danlee and Mazama townsite! Mazama's heart is DANLEE MINE, the eleven richest claims of the district, a statement backed up by the first assays made of typical ores, indicating SHIPPING VALUES at the surface of a number of the outcroppings! This prospect has EVERYTHING: Accessibility; Cheap Transportation; Equable Climate; High Values; Extensive Ore Veins; and Favorable Lease for a Three-Generation Period. Lastly: NOW IS THE HEY-DEY OF GOLD! Nations without Gold are voting bonuses for its production. The World is crying for more of it, and it is the one article of trade which depression has ENHANCED in value instead of depreciating!

of the Danlee Mine. It was owned by Mr. Hotchkiss but leased to Dan Carrol and Lee Ferral. The mine was billed as a *"Cow pasture that camouflaged gold."* During spring and early summer, a great effort was under way to promote this enterprise, climaxing in a giant free barbecue celebrating the shipment of the first carload of ore from the mine. It was reported that the largest crowd ever assembled in Mazama attended the gala occasion. Between 1,250 and 1,500 people showed up and 267 cars were parked at the Danlee mine. Some question existed as to whether any ore was actually shipped, but considerable stock in the mine was sold that day.

Surrounding mines, the Azurite, Gold Hill, Flagg, and Mazama Queen, were back in operation. Additionally, a store had been opened. The *Journal* reported, *"This time however,* [the store] *comes into a thriving farming community instead of a wilderness."* The 1930 census reported that 166 persons and 35 farms were included in the precinct. This number did not include the people living in the new homes which had been built during the last year of the latest mining activity.

The spring of 1932 saw a flurry of mining activity and, quite contrary to the economy of the rest of the country, things seemed to be booming in Mazama. The owners of the Mazama Queen Mine near Goat Wall Creek, which would employ fifteen men, planned to start operations soon. It was reported in the *Journal:*

"A new extraction process had been discovered and a new company had been formed of men from Seattle and the county. They already had a compressor and drill on site and were expecting 18 tons of equipment to arrive and be in operation by mid-May. A tunnel had been driven a distance of 410 feet into an immense ore body and with the mine location right on the hiway a few miles from Mazama, costs for extraction should be relatively low."

However, progress did not go quite as fast as predicted at the Mazama Queen. It was June before the machinery for the electric power plant could be installed along with an electric hoist at the head of a tramway. After a test run, it was discovered that a new type of furnace would be needed. But despite the setbacks, a run had been made at the Mazama Queen by the end of June, with values of $80 per ton reported. Considering that the price of gold was around $20 per ounce, that was not a bad figure.

January, 1932, also saw the death of Charles Ballard — miner, engineer, and designer of towns. Ballard's dreams and predictions for the Slate Creek mines did not die along with him, however. After laying idle for thirty years, the Indiana Mine came to life in 1935 under the management of owner F.D. Hyde, who made his headquarters at the Hotel Winthrop. A small crew of men worked the site and by September had completed a 500-foot cableway from the Indiana tunnel to the floor of the basin.

Hyde was a New York railroad construction contractor, but was familiar with the area. Thirty years earlier, at the time of the Slate Creek boom, three railroads were racing their surveys into the district. Hyde's partner and engineer directed the survey for the Canadian road up the Pasayten over Windy Pass and down Slate Creek. As a result of this, Parker & Hyde acquired claims in the divide. At that time, Hyde authorized a sawmill to be built and lumber was cut for a power plant and mine buildings. That same year, 1905, the power lines were run to the Indiana basin and the Eureka Mill on the North Fork of Slate Creek. The Chancellor plant furnished power for two seasons, but when no railroad showed up and activities died, it was decided to patent the Chancellor holdings. Thus it was that Hyde returned years later to continue a dream he had begun many years before.

The temporary closure of the Mazama Queen Mine in March, 1932, raised a bit of apprehension in the upper valley. This subsided when in June it was announced that the Mazama Queen was now the Continental Gold & Silver Com-

pany and the new mine was *"one of the best equipped mine plants in the Northwest, though at present is only of 50 ton capacity."*

To say that mining was an economic factor, or that there had been apprehension, needs to be put in the proper perspective. Many in the community participated in mining, but frequently there was no pay. Men would work and be paid for a few weeks or months and then, when the money ran out, would be promised

High up on Goat Wall to the southeast of Goat Wall Creek, the Mazama Queen Mine operated on and off for some years. It was obviously not very accessible. A cable way and basket brought ore to the mill at the bottom, but men scrambled up the cliff the hard way. This photo shows two men working, one at the bottom of the ladder and the other on the right.

stock or cash when the mine paid. The major revenue was the sale of stock in the mines. The promoters made some money from the stock sales, and workers were paid to *"dig a little further,"* start a new mine, or reopen an abandoned or bankrupt claim. The few mines in the Mazama area that actually took out any amounts of gold are said to have *"put any profits back into the mine."*

An exception to the disappointing pattern of small mines was the Azurite Mine, a major mining operation which ran year-round for many years in the 1930s and was located in the mountains on Mill Creek. But by 1938, even the Azurite quit. It had produced $972,000 in gold and silver over the years, but was $120,000 short of its total investment. By 1942, the owner, ASARCO, had removed most of the equipment of value from the site.

According to Bill Wehmeyer, *"the only guys that made any money from a little mine were Fred and Henry Dammann."* Henry Dammann was born in 1879 and came from Germany as a young boy on a sailing ship, like many turn-of-the-century immigrants. He started on the west coast and worked his way east by working in the mines or at any other job he could find. According to Bill, Fred and Hank had a placer mine in the creek and dug a hole and put up a cabin above it. They decided to put in a root cellar by digging in the hill behind their cabin hauling the dirt out through the front door. Part way through the root cellar they hit a little pocket and took out about seven thousand dollars in gold. Henry eventually claimed a homestead in the Methow, but

spent a big part of his profit from the gold strike bringing his family and relatives from Germany to America.

Road Building, an Economic Priority

As dreams of prosperous mines continued, so did dreams of a North Cross State Highway. By the end of 1935, federal money was approved to build a road from Diablo to Azurite and Slate Creek. This was a significant departure from the Cascade Pass route into which so much effort and time had been invested. The decision came as a great shock to many. The federal government sent WPA crews to start a mine-to-market road from Diablo to Azurite. Whatcom County would work with the federal people to run a road up Granite Creek and the East Fork, and then over to Slate Creek. If money was available, the road would run up the existing road to the New Light Mine and over Harts Pass.

The year 1938 was just like every other year since 1890 so far as news and interest in a North Cross State Highway was concerned. The headline in the May 12 edition of the *Journal* said *"Ruby Creek Road to be Built, 1939 May See Thru Traffic To Coast by Northern Route."* The pursuit of the highway was an unending battle. It was the object of countless meetings, committees, trips to the State Capitol, and the platform of nearly everyone running for public office in North Central Washington. Attempts were made at both the state and county levels. The problem was not only getting the money for the highway, but also in determining the route.

By the late 1930s, engineering and construction capabilities allowed roads to be built just about anywhere. The location thus became more of a political compromise than a question of construction feasibility. The question of location remained unresolved as the 1930s came to a close.

Chapter 6

The 1940s and 1950s - Cattle Ranches Grow, The War Strikes, And The River Floods

Beef cattle became a bigger part of the ranching scene in Mazama during the 1940s. By this time, the more persistent and harder working farmers had begun to accumulate more land. The first generation of homesteaders was ready to retire or their children had left the farms for better jobs elsewhere. This often made possible the purchase of neighboring lands at a reasonable price, and with the larger pieces of land, beef cattle could be raised if a rancher could also acquire grazing rights on nearby Forest Service lands. There still existed the problem of shipping cattle to market, but with the improved roads and better trucks, hauling to markets as far away as Seattle became a common practice.

Albert Ventzke of Rockview was an original homesteader who managed to put together three ranches totaling 360 acres. Albert and his brother, Emil, came the year after the area had opened for homesteads and camped on Bear Creek. They were shown around by Ben Pearrygin who recommended to them the land at the mouth of Cub Creek, where Emil Ventzke took up a claim, and in Rockview, where Albert located in 1888. The men took the first wagons beyond the forks of the Methow and Chewuck Rivers.

Other residents also began to combine homesteads into larger tracts. For example, Calloway Cassal put together HES 94, 197, and 198. Jack Stewart put several ranches together between Goat Creek and Mazama on the north side of the river, and Don Shafer had about 450 acres in HES 91, 92, and 93. A number of people who had dairy herds began adding or switching to beef cattle.

Notes in the *Methow Valley Journal* in the spring of 1941 give a flavor of what was happening in Mazama at the time:

- *"Andy Russell is hauling beef cattle to the Seattle Market for Paul Heaton of Winthrop, making 3 trips this week."*
- *"Jack Wehmeyer took a truck load of cattle to Seattle this week and Mrs. Wehmeyer accompanied him."*
- *"At round up last fall Calloway Cassal failed to find 6 head. Stock usually doesn't survive in the severe winters of this country, but this week he found 2 yearlings in a protected spot at the forks of Boulder Creek. They had managed to find food enough to keep alive but were very thin. He also found the skeleton of a cow he lost."*
- *"Roy Kumm has installed electrical equipment in his dairy barn and separator house."*

Don and Dorothy Shafer were new arrivals in the 1940s. The Shafers had been raising cows in Edmonds, north of Seattle. At first, they raised dairy cows, and later switched to beef cattle. However, they needed a bigger ranch if they were going to get into beef cattle on a major scale. Don had hunted deer in Mazama in the 1930s and it was the first place he wanted to go to expand their operation.

In 1945, the Shafers bought HES 92 and 93 from the Short family. Don doubled the size of the field on HES 92. He was a good mechanic, loved machinery, and was one of the first in the upper valley to use a "cat" for farming. Most Mazama farmers still used horses even in the 1940s and felt that something like a cat was too slow. Don hooked up several discs and equipment and in one pass with the cat did what would take many days to accomplish with a team. The next year, a number of Mazama farmers wanted to hire Don to do their field work. The first year the Shafers put up hay in a mound, but the second year they got a baler and were the first in Mazama to have baled hay.

———————

Another development during the 1940s was in recreation. As an economic factor, it was expanding beyond the hunting and fishing for which the area was noted. On the Chewuck River, the Spaeth family had opened the Methow Valley Ranch, a dude ranch that received considerable recognition. *Sunset Magazine* carried the note that *"The METHOW VALLEY RANCH of Winthrop will stay open this winter to take ski dudes."* Skiing grew in popularity during the 1940s. The season of 1940-41 had been a glorious one for snow and enthusiasm was high.

The Forest Service and the CCC constructed a ski hill on the mountain side southwest of Patterson Lake. It was within easy driving distance of Upper Methow towns. During January and February, 560 names appeared in the ski hill registry located at the warming hut on the bottom of the ski hill. The figure did not, however, accurately represent the actual number of persons who visited the hill as many visitors failed to register. Twenty-eight towns were represented in the registry, and on the biggest day, sixty-eight people registered. The Forest Service considered widening the road to the area and cooperated with the high school ski club in clearing the hill. Plans were also made to build a lodge to replace the temporary shelter. The plans were tentative but were sent to the Forest Service in Portland for approval. The lodge would have a kitchen, a front porch, a full basement, a fireplace, and a balcony.

———————

No discussion of life anywhere in America in the 1940s would be complete without touching on the effect of the war on the community. As in every town in America, the threat of war and the actual start of war overshadowed nearly everything else in the valley, particularly things such as ski lodges. The CCC camps and men had been swallowed up by the Army and all the local young men had registered for the draft.

A 1942 headline in the paper said *"Boys at Head of Winthrop Class Plan To Enter Army,"* and went on to tell about the boys. Jim Erickson, valedictorian, was student body president, active in skiing and football. He planned to become a flying cadet. During his spare time he managed a ranch and milked twelve cows before and after school. Howard Brewer was salutatorian, athletic manager, a member of the student council, and had achieved honors in skiing. His plan was to work for the Forest Service during the summer before entering the Army.

Members of the community joined forces to help with the war effort. In January of 1942, the Mazama ladies met at the Forest Service warehouse for Red Cross sewing and planned to meet again that month at the home of Mrs. Roy Kumm. Mr. and Mrs. Rufus Blevins joined thousands of others as air raid spotters who staffed towers up and down the West Coast. The Forest Service moved the Blevins to Slate Peak, where they remained for the duration of the war.

Support groups were formed to help those who remained at home cope with fears of loved ones at war. For example, the Navy Mothers' Club formed and met monthly. Men home on leave were treated with great respect and buying war bonds was the major promotion of the day. The September 22, 1944, issue of the *Methow Valley News* carried a full page ad for the *"1st ANNUAL METHOW VALLEY SPORTSMAN ASSOC. DANCE IN THE SPACIOUS WINTHROP AUDITORIUM. Tickets $1. A FREE WAR BOND WILL BE GIVEN ...all profit to be used in furthering our interests in wildlife and game in the valley."*

In 1942, a group of the community's most progressive citizens joined together to help promote the Methow and attract business and tourists. One of the first tasks was to get twenty-eight miles of road built on Harts Pass to connect to the coast. The group included:

George Zahn; R.E. Mansfield; Tom Weborn from Pateros; and George Dibble, Jerry Sullivan, and W.F. Burge from Winthrop. The group became known as the Methow Valley Chamber of Commerce, or MVCC. Ironically, years later the same letters would be used to identify a group whose goals and principles were quite different from those of the MVCC of the 1940s.

Jack Wilson

Jack Wilson arrived in the 1940s and purchased HES 84 and 250 on Early Winters Creek. Jack was a self-made man who had been a steel worker on the Golden Gate Bridge and a shipyard worker in Vancouver.

Jack had married a pretty model named Elsie Wheeler and they came to Mazama for a different way of life. Jack felt there was just about nothing he couldn't do if he put his mind to it, and he set about building cabins for a resort. He built barns and corrals and bought a few

Jack Wilson

horses, and like most men in Mazama, worked for Hazard Ballard's outfit to learn the packing business. When Hazard's wife, Zora, eventually had to get out of the packing business after her husband's death, Jack stepped in and gradually purchased harnesses, horses, and equipment from her. By 1949, Zora had turned over her hunting parties to Jack. With this business and the blessings of Mrs. Ballard combined with Wilson's drive and Elsie's charm, the Wilsons' Early Winters Resort got off to a good start.

Jack continued building his cabins and expanding his pack string, and did odd jobs on the side to earn money to buy furnishings and materials for the cabins. He bid on trail contracts for the Forest Service and trapped in the winter. Jack was a whirlwind of activity and understood the need for promotion of both his business and the valley. Jack loved the mountains, the valley and the wilderness and wanted to share it with all who would listen or come and experience its beauty. He was active in the Sportsman's Council and the Chamber of Commerce, and was a promoter of the North Cross State Highway Association.

In contrast to all this business, Jack also had the ability to take a person into the back country wilderness in an atmosphere of peace and tranquillity, to melt into nature and become a part of it. During the next three decades, Jack would become friends with and have clients who were mayors, governors, Congressmen, the Chief Justice of the U.S. Supreme Court, billionaires, and captains of industry.

Andy Russell was another enterprising Mazama resident who did what he could to get by. He farmed and logged and tried his hand at the restaurant business by opening a cafe and gas pump at the Mazama corners, the junction of Highway 20 and Mazama Road (see page 32). The most notable thing about the business was its shape — two curved rooms connected with a rectangular structure. It is alleged to have been built from the forms of a coffer dam on the Columbia. Andy was a junk collector, so it is quite likely that these rumors were true. The cafe was called the "Do Drop Inn" and operated on and off for several years, along with a Shell gas pump. Andy and his wife had it for only about a year after it opened. According to the *News*, it changed hands in 1947 to Mr. & Mrs. Clyde Alexander from Bremerton, Washington.

———————

In addition to World War II, another major event of the 1940s was the flood of 1948. Many events in the Methow are referred to as having occurred either before or after "the '48 flood." It is mentioned in the recollections of several older residents. One story recalled by a witness tells of a mishap involving a citizen of Winthrop known for his heavy drinking. After an evening of drinking in Winthrop, the citizen decided to accompany Knute Pearson to his home in Mazama. It was the first night of the high water, and when the pair got to the Weeman Bridge, the approaches were under water. They got stuck, but eventually made it through.

The next morning, however, the citizen was found walking down the road in water running knee-deep. Weeman Bridge was gone so he was headed down the Wolf Creek road to get a drink in Winthrop. The water was waist-high across the road past the Morrow place and the citizen was washed out to the middle of the river. He grabbed a log that was floating by and was washed all the way to the Sunny M (Dr. Blende's Dude Ranch) where, luckily, a man on a horse had been roping. The horseman waded out, threw him a rope, and pulled him in.

Zora Ballard's Diary

After Hazard Ballard died in 1938, his wife, Zora, continued to run the packing and horse business from their Lost River home on HES 97. Hazard and Zora played major roles in the development of both Rockview and the Robinson/Lost River area. Although they were involved in many enterprises such as the building and operation of the Rockview Mill, the business venture that lasted the longest for the Ballards was tourism. From the time the Ballards took over the Hotel

and Last Chance Saloon in Robinson, they were in some form of the tourist business or another.

Zora kept a diary in her later years, and although the entries are mostly day-to-day domestic activities, she also tells her view of two events that became part of Mazama history. The excerpts below are just as Zora wrote them. People mentioned in the diary entries are as follows: Jerry is Edna Farrar, caretaker in Chancellor during the 1940s; Roma Johnson is Zora's brother; Jimmie Sparks is a close friend and sort of an adopted son to Zora; and Sam is probably Sam Bodie, a friend of Hazard and Jack Wilson from the coast.

The first event chronicled in Zora's diary began when Edna "Jerry" Farrar had notified someone (possibly Jimmie Sparks)

Zora and Hazard Ballard at their Lost River home(82). This picture was probably taken in the 1920s. Hazard had mined in the Slate Creek area, built a portion of Harts Pass Road, operated the Robinson Hotel, owned and operated the Rockview sawmill, and built up a packing and outfitting business. Hazard died in 1938, but Zora continued to operate the packing business with the help of her brother, Roma Johnson, for another 10 years.

that she was leaving from Chancellor. She asked Jimmie to meet her and drive her out. Zora's diary contains the following entries.

Oct. 18 [1947], Sat.: *Anderson left 9 PM. Sam and friend came 9 PM and went up to meet Jerry, couldn't make it so Jimmie went up with Jeep but saw no one, she was to wait at pass but did not get there. Rained terribly.*

Oct. 19, Sun.: *Jimmie, Sam and young man went again to pass in jeep to look out, walked on 1 mile. 4 hrs snow 3 feet deep worn out came back know nothing of Jerry. Hope she is safe, raining tonight again. Sam left for home. After supper Dents packed out by Roma and Ray 2:30 PM.*

Oct. 20, Mon.: *Early Breakfast saddled horses for trip to Robinson and Weeman Cr. Harley went to get Bouldron & Bells. Roma after 2 men on Weeman Cr. Jimmie & 5 men to pass. Found Jerry dead by the road side. Hard trip to carry her out. Poor Angus would not follow. Poor Jerry, her beloved mountains took her life.*

Oct. 21, Tues.: *Ray went to bring Angus out, he followed, Wright will keep him.*

Oct. 23, Thur.: *Went to Twisp, Anna had fine dinner ready for us, Lydea there. We all went to church at 2 PM, Jerry had nice service, flowers beautiful. Dear girl rest in peace.*

The October 23, 1947, issue of the *Methow Valley News* carried the story that Zora chronicled on a daily basis above. The *News* headline read *"Edna Coffin Farrar Meets Death on Snowy Harts Pass Trail."* The story continued:

"Found dead Sunday was Edna Farrar age 60. She was coming from Chancellor to Harts Pass where arrangements had been made to meet her. Due to heavy snow and failure of her to appear as arranged caused the party to go back and prepare to go after her. The Highway department cleared the way for a search party Monday morning and a party of 5 from Mazama made their way through 3 feet of snow up Harts Pass. The search party consisted of Ellis Peters, Bill Pederson, and Clyde Alexander. It was found she wore no snow shoes and her tracks were found beyond the spot where she was found, indicating she had started to return to her cabin. Apparently tired from the struggle thru the deep snow, she was found sitting by the trail and it is believed she was a victim of heart failure. Mr. Farrar, who worked at the New Light Mine died in 1946. She worked as a government meteorologist. She was reported to know the country well and was a active hiker who thought nothing of carrying a 75-pound pack."

Another series of entries in Zora's diary told of the 1948 flood as she experienced it from her home in Lost River.

May 24 [1948], Mon.: *Mr. Green came to phone about Goat Wall Creek washing out road and had called Ray [probably Ray Patterson, assistant Ranger at the Early Winters station] about trees against Lost River Bridge. State men came and pulled them out, also built bridge over Wall Creek.*

May 25, Tues.: *Looked at river at 6 AM.*

May 27, Thur.: *River high, thunder, power off at 10:30.*

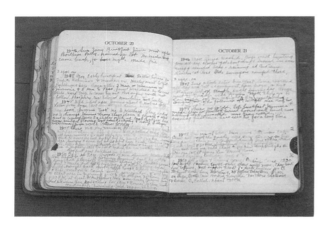

In later years, without her husband, Zora Ballard's diary seemed to become an important part of her life. She never failed to confide in it, or to record in its pages the events of the day and important matters in her life.

May 28, Fri.: *Raining, bridge gone, water higher. Hope Mr. Cutler* [who lived across Lost River] *has plenty of food. Power off but came on at 8 AM for 15 min. Jimmie took jeep down below Wall Creek. Flooded everywhere. Island all gone by evening. No lights until 10 PM, no news, no mail.*

May 29, Sat.: *Water running along hill below grade, all the trees gone on each side of where bridge was, fill going also, drift formed up stream. Water half way to Cutler's in road. Still raining most of night, no power, no phone. Green came up, Jimmie went down to get dog feed if bridge is still in at Mazama .*

May 30, Sun.: *River fell some, lots of drift along sides. Jimmie gone to Wilsons' but Mazama bridge partly gone. 6 bridges out on Methow and many houses washed away at Twisp, no power or phone, food shortage & very little gas. News over battery radio.*

May 31, Mon.: *River falling, island forming where bridge was.*

June 1, Tues.: *Jimmie and Mr. Green built bridge over Wall Creek.*

June 3, Thur.: *Jimmie, Alva & Mr. Green put line across river for Mr. Cutler to get mail.*

June 9, Wed.: *Still no power or phone yet. Listen to prize fight on radio.*

June 10, Thur.: *Goat Creek bridged now.*

June 13, Sun.: *Wilson visited, went by Weeman bridge. Rained hard.*

June 24, Thur.: *Jimmie worked several days on bridge, Mr. Cutler crossed tonight with his car.*

Zora Ballard died in 1956. Always well regarded, active in the community, wife of a leader and entrepreneur, Zora lived a full life. Her diary reveals, however, that her later years were not among her happiest. She treated Jimmy Sparks as a son and her life revolved around him. She cooked for him and kept house with the expectation that he would act as a son and respond to her kindness. However, he wouldn't show up for meals and vanished for days without telling her. Some felt that he took advantage of Zora, and she spent her last years worrying about him.

As the 1950s came to an end, the Winthrop main street was still a functional junction in the road. The major grocery store, Shafer's Hardware & General Store, and the Pool Hall were all within a minute's walk.

Chapter 7

The 1960s - Big Valley Ranch, Early Winters Resort and Edelweiss

The 1960s brought new faces and new projects to the area. Although it was the beginning of another chapter in Mazama history, the early 1960s continued to deal with the transition mood of the 1950s. The ethic of conquering the wilderness remained. The decades-old momentum of building a community and attracting new settlers was alive and well at Mazama. Attracting industry was a goal equal to providing public education on early settlers' lists of priorities. This was an ethic throughout the entire West during the early years of development, but it had hung on a little longer in this remote part of the state.

By the end of the 1950s and the beginning of the 1960s, the decades of work aimed at bringing the North Cross State Highway to reality was at its height. It was a political matter to get funds for the project, and publicity was an important tool in the political arena. Methow people were good at this and they concocted an event which fit their style and brought attention to their cause. Jack Wilson, an avid highway booster, was one of the chief organizers of the event and provided much of the stock and equipment needed.

Residents staged a Pony Express-type ride over the proposed route of the new highway from Diablo Dam to Early Winters. *The Seattle Times* reported that *"Jerry Sullivan, a strong silent-type cowboy from Winthrop, raced from Diablo Dam, across the Cascade Mountains to Early Winters, exhausting eight horses on a rough rain-drenched eight-hour gallop. Fresh mounts were stationed at relay points along the 55-mile up and down route."*

Rider Jerry Sullivan is congratulated at the end of his ride by two early boosters of the North Cross State Highway, Les Holloway and George Zahn.

Summing up the day-long effort, Sullivan said, *"Just goes to show why we need this road. If you took available highways you couldn't have made the trip as fast by car."*

An old-fashioned community barbecue capped the events of the day for the Mazama and Winthrop enthusiasts.

Getting the North Cross State Highway funded, started, and built was still a major community issue, but most of the new settlers to the valley were people looking for an alternative to industry and belching smoke stacks. The Puget Sound basin was growing fast and while the Methow was still a six or seven hour trip from Seattle, it was considered by many to be only a few years away from discovery by the masses.

The Mazama Store in the late 1960s, while it was still run by Bill and Vi Pederson.

Harold and Tina Heath

Harold Heath was a self-made man and an industrialist in the true sense of the word. Based in Seattle, he had built an empire which got its start serving the aircraft industry. Heath Techna manufactured the interiors for commercial aircraft. The firm expanded into diversified industries and the company's stock was actively traded publicly. Harold was a wealthy business tycoon with all the advantages

and disadvantages that accompany such a position in society.

One of the negatives of Harold's position was the resulting stress and the need to escape from the constant pressures of business. To this end, Harold frequented the finest resorts, spas, and retreats only to find, however, that instead of relaxing, he was in a social whirl, getting dressed up, meeting people, and staying up late. He had to find a spot to really get away. On a business trip to the Okanogan he asked an associate if he knew of a place that was like the Okanogan but with trees. His friend suggested the Methow. On this suggestion, Harold met real estate agents Lewis Cooley and Grace Walsh.

Harold purchased the Golden Doe Ranch in 1963 and the Big Buck ranch in 1965. In 1966, he bought 1,500 acres in the valley bottom near the inter-city airport. The next year, he bought 1,200 acres in Rockview from the McCauley family. The property consisted of the Albert Ventzke place, the original H.H. Johnson homestead, some of the Wehmeyer homesteads, and other land that had been assembled by the Cooper family.

The same year, Harold bought the 160-acre Boesel place, and the following year he purchased 220 acres from

Holcomb and a large piece by the river from Gamble Lumber Co. Finally, in 1972 Harold bought the last 120-acre piece and completed what he called the "Big Valley Ranch." Along with this massive acquisition, Harold and Lewis Cooley, who owned the bank in Twisp, were also buying up orchards.

Harold hired managers for the ranches. He hired a local man, Jim McCauley, to manage the Big Valley Ranch. Jim in turn hired Jim Holcomb as his assistant. Together they ran a cow and calf operation on a fairly big scale by Methow Valley standards. They had lots of hay and pasture lands, plenty of range, and the money to buy good machines and equipment.

Two significant events brought Harold's buying spree to a halt. First, Mother Nature produced the winter of 1967-68 with record low temperatures in the valley of 50 degrees below zero. The season destroyed many of Harold's orchards and this part of his business suffered a $750,000 loss. Next, a recession tumbled the price of Heath Techna shares from $120 a share to $7 a share, and finally to a low of $1 per share. Harold was forced to liquidate his holdings to cover the loans he had taken to acquire them. One by one, he sold off his holdings at bargain prices. He combined operations and cut expenses as best he could. As if this weren't bad enough luck, at about the same time, Harold's home in south Seattle burned to the ground.

In 1970, Harold and his wife, Tina, left the area and returned to Cincinnati, Ohio, to start over. Art Davis looked after the ranch while they were gone, and Aaron Burkhart leased it until 1982, when Harold and Tina returned and resumed operation of the ranch themselves. Harold and Tina dove into the community. Tina was elected to the school board and was part of the Mazama Advisory Committee working on the community master plan. Harold bought 500 yearling calves and got into the cattle business once again. Harold tried until 1985 to raise calves to yearlings on the ranch and sell them. Unfortunately, this venture was not profitable. Harold turned to leasing the pasture, at so many dollars per cow/calf pair. He continued leasing into the 1990s.

In 1991, the Washington Wildlife and Recreation Coalition lobbied the state legislature for money to buy the part of the ranch situated in the valley. The Coalition obtained the money and purchased the land from Harold and Tina, on the condition that they would remain on the ranch grazing cattle. The Coalition wanted to preserve the land as pasture and open space and to prevent its development. From 1991 on, Harold continued to pasture cattle on the ranch under a 5-year lease with the Coalition. As long as Harold continues to use the land as pasture, the Coalition will continue to renew the lease.

The Coalition's purchase of Harold's land was a wonderful gift to the valley and those who love it. However, as with any decision of significant impact, there are some who, although fully aware of the benefit to the area, questioned the propriety of spending public funds in this manner. Nonetheless, the purchase of the land ensured the preservation of the open fields and view corridors, which have become a sort of "signature" of the Upper Methow Valley.

Wilson's Resort in the 1960s

Young riders, guests at Early Winters Resort, ride the dirt road which today is Highway 20.

In the mid 1960s, development of the Early Winters Resort began to hit its stride. Jack Wilson had stopped building additional buildings and Elsie Wilson was running the resort. She cleaned the cabins, did the laundry in the wash house, kept the accounts, handled reservations, and supervised a wrangler who helped with the horses and rides.

Jack did the maintenance, ran the pack trips, managed the marketing, and did the dreaming. Things weren't all rosy though. Jack had been doing some trail contracting and had lost a bundle of money. He had a way of thinking a job was easier than it actually turned out to be, and under-bid on some big sections of trail construction. He was in debt to the bank and the bank was calling the loan.

Jack was making some money by packing hunters and fishermen and the wilderness trip business he had developed. Elsie's work at the cabins made it a profitable business, but not profitable enough to pay off the debt Jack had established in his trail building fiasco. Fortunately, Jack was able to borrow from Mrs. Kay Wagner, an old friend, and staved off the bank's foreclosure efforts. Money problems didn't seem to bother Jack very much, however. He once bought a horse and knew he would be in trouble with Elsie. So, he named the horse "Hay" and gave Elsie the bill to pay as an expense.

Elsie would worry and fret, but Jack went on dreaming and planning bigger and better things, such as building the North Cross State Highway, the promotion of the Methow, the management of the wilderness area, and the operation of the Washington State Department of Game. The Department of Game was one of Jack's pet peeves. While his objectives were nearly the same as the agency's — the enhancement of wildlife — he felt the state bureaucrats didn't have a clue about game management, and said so in no uncertain terms.

At about this time, Jack began to figure out how he could make some money during the winter. His was strictly a summer and fall operation. During the first few winters he spent in Mazama, he trapped. He would snow-shoe miles up Early Win-

Jack and Elsie Wilson raised an orphaned fawn whose mother was killed on the highway.

ters Creek and stay in a small log shelter (located where Lone Fir Campground is today) and trap the creeks that flow into Early Winters.

Eventually, when the price of hides had dropped, but the difficulty of trapping remained the same, Jack pondered the possibility of winterizing the cabins and catering to skiers. There was a nice little ski hill behind the cabins. In addition to skiing, Jack could offer sleigh rides and people could snowshoe around the fields and up the trails along Early Winters Creek. (At the time, cross country skiing in this area was virtually nonexistent except as a competition sport.) Jack shared his idea with Doug Devin, a long time friend and summer guest of the resort.

Doug was in the ski business. He had been active in the establishment of Crystal Mountain and was a supervisor in the ski school there. He was also in the ski equipment part of the industry as a retailer,

wholesaler, and manufacturer. Doug was aware of the need for more ski facilities in the state if the sport was going to continue to grow. He also had an idea of what was necessary for a successful ski resort. He knew that the hill behind the cabins, where Jack considered putting a simple lift, had only a few hundred feet of vertical drop and would not justify anything more than a beginner hill. When he told Jack this probably would not work, they got out maps and began looking at other possibilities. Doug and Jack found that around the corner was a north-facing hill with 4,000 feet of drop and variable terrain.

This appeared too good to be true. Jack arranged for an inspection trip that fall. Doug was more than a little impressed with what they had discovered and set about gathering more information that

This trapper's cabin, now located at the Early winters Ranger Station, was moved from the Lone fir Campground area where it had been used for many years by men trapping in the Early Winters area. Jack Wilson was one of these men and was probably the last to stay overnight in the shelter in mid-winter.

would be needed, such as snow depths, temperatures, weather conditions, snow characteristics, and the availability of private property at the base of the hill. Doug felt that this last factor, the availability of private property, was most essential. He shared his findings and opinions with several colleagues in the ski industry and all concurred that if a feasibility study could be completed and the results were favorable, a first class ski area in Washington state could become a reality. Skiers and industry people had always recognized that a high quality ski area would probably need to be on the east slope of the Cascades to get the weather and snow quality that people traveled to the Rocky Mountains to find. They also knew that private property was necessary to help finance a resort and make available accommodations and year-round activity.

Devin enlisted the support and enthusiasm of Len Miller, a neighbor of Wilson's and owner of HES 89 and 90, property which would be critical in any development plan. Len was an active skier, avalanche consultant, and photographer, skills useful in the completion of the feasibility study. It was a totally volunteer effort. Len and Doug formed the "Methow Valley Winter Sports Council" comprised of a combination of Methow Valley community leaders and experienced ski industry people. Doctor Bill Henry and his wife, Ann, were skiers and active in the valley community. Bill acted as chairman of the council. Lew Cooley was the banker in Twisp and acted as treasurer

and undertook the task of raising money to help cover expenses. Ski industry notables included Jack Nagel, former Olympian and head of the Crystal Mountain Ski School; Mike Ewing, professional ski patrolman from Vail; and Bob Cram, a writer, illustrator and host of a weekly television ski show in Seattle.

This group along with others made a major assault on the mountain equipped with cameras, altimeters, slope-meters, and measuring devices. It was the first major effort to obtain good information and expert opinions. Len Miller had already made a couple of trips to the summit, although not with the feasibility study in mind, and found the best route up and good ski runs down.

Preliminary mountain studies along with snow and weather observations were made on snow shoe and snow-cat trips up the mountain and in the base area by volunteers including this trio. Left to right: Jack Wilson, Doug Devin, and Claude Miller.

This flurry of activity occurred in March, 1968, the winter of record low temperatures in the Methow and superb snow conditions. In January, Mazama recorded a temperature of 52 degrees below zero, the lowest temperature ever recorded in Washington state. As the skiers cruised down through meadows and a clear-cut, cameras filmed powder snow flying shoulder-high behind them and the rooster tail of snow evaporating almost entirely before it fell back to the ground. It was some of the best skiing these world-traveled skiing professionals had ever seen. The films were incorporated into a television show by Bob Cram and later made into a movie that was shown far and wide, telling of the ski potential on Sandy Butte at Early Winters.

Devin completed the feasibility study the next year, but even before it was finished, skiers and industry people were hearing about Early Winters in the Methow. This posed a serious problem for the group. If they were to attract a major firm or developer it would be next to impossible to gather all of the necessary land at a reasonable cost in the face of great speculation in land values.

It was also at this time that the Shafers approached their friend, Doug Devin, and asked him if he was interested in buying their land. A developer had been working with Dorothy Shafer to purchase their land to subdivide, but had made Dorothy mad in the process. The Shafers had bought property in the Columbia basin and wanted to move there. Doug said he would see what he could do. This probably precipitated Doug's next actions.

What was necessary was a group of people with money who would collect and "bank" the land so a resort developer would not have to outbid speculators for the important pieces necessary for the project. Finding people with money to invest in land who were willing to take a large risk and then turn the land over to another without maximizing their profit was not easy. It had to be people who saw the development of great skiing as equal to, or more important than, profiting from a good investment.

Doug found such individuals in his associates in the ski industry and at Crystal Mountain — directors and the Chairman of Crystal Mountain, the former owners of A&T Ski Company (a large national pioneer ski manufacturer based in Seattle), and a group of ski instructors. This group purchased the Shafer ranch, HES 91, 92, and 93, and then over a period of time purchased the land owned by Len and Dianne Miller, HES 89 and 90.

There were a half dozen other smaller pieces from one to five acres in size that proved to be difficult to purchase, as each owner thought he was in a powerful position to get a big price or be a hold-out and demand an enormous ransom. In addition, the Millers were starting to market a 36-lot subdivision which had to be stopped and the owners satisfied. It was a difficult and time-consuming task that Doug worked at for several years.

By the end of 1969, the Winter Sports Council had met with the Forest Service and told them of their activities. The Forest Service indicated it had also been aware of Sandy Butte as a good ski potential and had listed it to be considered in future studies.

Edelweiss

While the planning was going on at Early Winters, a large second home development called Edelweiss, was underway across the valley on the hillside up river from the Weeman Bridge. The owners advertised hundreds of lots from one-half to two acres complete with underground power and water. Camping areas by the river and plans for a community swimming pool were drawing cards to encourage purchasers.

Bill Laney, a Seattle insurance executive, and Norm Hamilton, an orchardist, had fallen in love with the Valley and put together partners to purchase the land from Aaron Burkhart. It was the largest and most ambitious project of this type ever tried in the upper valley, and Bill and his partners planned to create a development which would be environmentally sensitive but still modestly profitable. In 1963 Bill got into the deal because he just wanted a place to build a summer cabin. He called George Dibble, a banker in Winthrop, who suggested he talk to Aaron Burkhart, who might have a piece of land for sale. Bill ended up buying 550 acres for $120,000 and entered the land development business.

Bill and Norm hired Don Drake as General Manager and started on the first of four plats that would eventually be developed under a set of covenants and restrictions patterned after Seattle's Windermere District. The first plat consisted of lots on the river and camp sites located in the floodplain, which sold for $2,400 with 10% down. The second plat consisted of 80 lots of 1 or 2 acres on the benches above the river and committed the project to installing a water and underground power system.

By now the project was costing big money and the development partners were scrambling to obtain financing. Lots were not selling well enough to cover the cash flow requirement, and for two years in the early 1970s, the county road on that side of the river was closed for construction. Sales during this time were a disaster. In addition to the road problem, the economy in the Seattle area was doing poorly, the partners were $200,000 in debt, and Norm Hamilton was unable to put any more money into the project.

The project was headed for bankruptcy. Bill had sold his business to cover part of the debt, but with no sales and no market, they were still in trouble. Through Bill's family, he was able to borrow enough money to keep going, but still had to sell some lots. He went to The Johns Company, a firm of former servicemen operating in Okinawa which sold investments to servicemen on a payroll deduction plan. It seemed to be a good combination. Bill liked the firm, and the firm's salesmen were excited about the project after a visit to the site.

It worked. The entire inventory of lots sold within 12 months. The sales company got all of the 20% down payments and Bill got the contracts. It was now the mid 1970s and with the new North Cascades Highway open, and the excitement about the potential ski area at Sandy Butte, the sales solved the cash flow problem. Within a few years, Edelweiss lots

were being resold by the original buyers
and nearly all made a nice profit on their
investments. But it would be a number of
years before Bill and his partners would
get their money back, and even longer
before they made even a modest profit.

A view of Mazama in the 1960s with Goat Peak snow still visible, which is a sign to old timers in Mazama that it is too early to plant the garden. The Mazama Ranch house and barns, visible here, and the surrounding area show little sign of change in the 30 intervening years.

Chapter 8

The 1970s - New Lifestyles and the Battle Over the Ski Resort

If there were specific events or dates that most affected Mazama and the Upper Methow, they would be the Slate Creek gold discovery in the 1890s and the opening of the North Cascades Highway in 1972. Of course, the Highway was not a surprise — it was under discussion for some seventy years and under construction for five.

As talk of the road construction began, as well as during and after construction, real estate sales in the Mazama area flourished. Subdivisions of every size were marketed, some by the older residents who had waited a lifetime to get a decent price for their land, but mostly by amateur speculators. Many one-acre lots were put on the market without too much success. One development called Bonanza Acres, on the Lost River Road (HES 197) divided acres of flood plain and attempted to sell the lots when the land was dry in late summer. Some lots were 100 feet wide and 900 feet long and reached from the road to the river and could be sold as 2-acre river front lots.

Generally, it was too early for lot buyers. Sales were to speculators, a few hunters, and people who dreamed of eventually moving to the valley, but few who discovered the beautiful upper Methow could afford to live or retire on an outside income. A few chose to live in Mazama and work in Winthrop, Twisp, or leave the valley for a few months at a time and then return.

By the 1970s, local industry was gone. There were no mining jobs, little local logging, and the sawmill had ceased operations. With a few exceptions, viable agriculture no longer existed. The Highway did bring the opportunity for the tourist and recreation industries to develop. Not everyone liked this, but the Methow Valley was now open to the world and

Early Winters Resort opened three cabins for winter use to attract cross-country skiers.

easily accessible. Thousands of travelers would pass over the spectacular North Cascades Highway and it was destined to become one of the state's major tourist attractions.

Lifestyle Changes in Mazama

The Methow Valley, like scores of other small Western communities and rural towns throughout the country, experienced what the old locals called a "hippie infestation" in the 1960s and 1970s. These so-called "hippies" came from everywhere, but California young folks seemed most prevalent next to those from western Washington. They moved into what seemed to be every house, shack, and cave in the area. Most meant well and were going to "live off the land" just as in the movies or in the nature books and magazines — a lifestyle so popular at that time.

A group moved into the house on HES 95 by Gate Creek until the house burned down. Another moved into the Welsh house on HES 91 with the plan of fixing it up and working for Don Shafer. They started by taking out the windows and doors and taking down part of the chimney. But when the weather got cold, the group, who hailed from southern California, vanished and the house never recovered. The cold Mazama winters forced most of the young newcomers, especially those without real houses in which to live, out of the valley or down the valley to Twisp.

Even with the winter exodus, the "hippie" population in the winter nearly equaled the native population. With great gusto, these folks entered into local activities such as the community potluck dinners and card parties, but their appetites often exceeded their contributions. Moreover, their contributions to the potlucks usually consisted of items such as tofu or organic apples, items not always appreciated by the palettes of old-time Mazama people. In spite of the different lifestyles, these new folks added spice to life in Mazama and were an important connection between Mazama and the outside world.

Even with the notoriety Mazama received during the 1970s and 1980s and all the real estate sales, the population didn't grow very much. It was sometimes even difficult to get enough able-bodied men to staff the volunteer fire truck. A women's auxiliary was eventually formed. A few summer homes were added but the number of voters in the Mazama precinct changed very little. Mazama seemed to be in suspense, waiting for some determination as to what, if anything, would be built at Early Winters.

Ski Industry Growth

The ski industry saw tremendous growth in the 1970s in ski equipment development as well as in resorts. Equipment that made skiing both easier to learn and safer for the participants brought tens of thousands of new skiers to the sport every year. Skiing became the "in" sport both in Europe and North America. Fashion and dining became an important element of the activity, and the concept of "skiing" broadened from merely a sport to nearly a lifestyle and a major economic generator and industry.

Towns and entire provinces in countries like Austria grew and flourished because of their location in the mountains and the quality of the skiing and hospitality offered. Virtual ghost towns in Colorado sprang to life if skiing was available, and old miners and ranchers on the verge of bankruptcy became wealthy.

Many individuals, as well as the state and several local governments in Washington, wanted to share in this prosperity. Oddly, most of the backers of skiing in the Methow, including founders of the Methow Winter Sports Council, were not motivated by the "get-rich" factor nor were they in any position to benefit much financially. Rather, these people were lovers of the sport and simply wanted a good place to ski closer to home than Colorado or Idaho. While a number of them bought real estate, it was to build a house for themselves rather than to buy on speculation of profit or resale. They were sportsmen and dreamers, not hard-nosed business developers. So, when these people went looking for funds and experienced individuals to build a major resort, they really didn't know where to turn or what to do.

A twenty-minute movie containing scenes of glorious powder snow skiing from Bob Cram's television ski show and summer activities filmed by Jeff Pritchard, a cinematography student at USC, constituted the main selling tool for Doug Devin. He purchased a second-hand movie projector which he lugged around along with the film and copies of the feasibility study, and talked to anyone who would listen. Sports Council members and ski industry people suggested persons to speak with and arranged interviews. Devin talked to Boise Cascade, a forest products company then into recreational real estate. He talked to a representative of the Teamsters Union Pension Fund looking for long-term investments who couldn't believe that there was not some hidden plan that would reap millions for Devin, and suggested that he might get a "cut."

Aspen Arrives

Vail, Colorado, was one of the great success stories of the early 1970s. A former employee of the area, Mike Ewing, now in the ski industry in Seattle, together with Devin's friend, Bob Parker, who was Vail's marketing manager, talked Vail management into taking a look at Early Winters. Flushed with success, Vail was looking for expansion possibilities. President Pete Seibert together with some of his staff made the trip to enjoy some of the good fishing in the Methow, but also to look over the other amenities the area had to offer.

About the same time Vail was considering expansion, the Aspen Skiing Corporation was doing the same. That company had also been quite successful and was looking for new ventures. Aspen was the older and larger firm at the time and was considerably more structured in its expansion efforts. It had assigned the task of finding ways to expand to its planning department, which began to actively look for new development opportunities from a list of nearly 300 possible sites.

Early Winters came to light from a list of Forest Service sites. Jerry Blann of Aspen contacted Devin for more information. The area looked good on paper and Aspen President Darcy Brown and Jerry Blann made several visits. They hired a helicopter and flew up, down, and around the mountain and base area and decided it was one of the best prospects they had seen to date.

Jerry Blann in 1975 community meetings.

Darcy, a former Colorado state legislator, had also been a cattle rancher in Colorado and Utah. He was a "country boy" at heart and had a feel for the rural values held by the residents of the Valley. He was honest and open, called things as they were, and was liked by all who came into contact with him. Jerry was 29 years old at the time and part of Aspen's planning department. He had grown up in the ski business. His father was the ski area manager at Mt. Bachelor in Bend, Oregon, and Jerry had been a young ski racer of note. Later in his career, Jerry would plan the Blackcomb Resort in Whistler, British Columbia, and become president of the Aspen Skiing Company.

The Aspen Skiing Company had a relatively active and prestigious Board of Directors. It included Robert McNamara, former Secretary of Defense; Paul Nitze, former Secretary of Navy and U.S. Chief United Nations Arms Negotiator; Bill Coors, owner of the Coors Brewing Company; and other prominent and affluent persons. After Darcy Brown and Jerry

Blann made their preliminary report, the Board approved pursuing the Early Winters site and obtaining options on real estate to allow base development to support the mountain. Jerry Blann was assigned to the project full time, and moved his family to the little house on HES 89 which Len Miller had built.

Jerry charged into the task of completing a detailed feasibility study and the preliminary design of the mountain. He hired scores of consultants and embarked on a state-of-the-art technical and environmental assessment of the area. This was 1975 and environmental planning was still a relatively new concept, especially for rural communities like the Methow. Tens of thousands of dollars were spent on studies of the water, air, transportation, geology, soils, and even archaeology.

Blann encouraged the county to expedite its planning and paid for Joe Porter, a planning specialist from Colorado, to assist. Doug Devin, acting as the chairman of the Citizens Land Use Advisory Committee, held dozens of public meetings to get community participation in drafting a comprehensive plan and zoning ordinance to prepare the community and the county for growth and to prevent strip development by speculators. A large factor in the adoption of a zoning ordinance was the education of the public to accept such law. Many parts of the county were very conservative and a great many citizens felt zoning was the forerunner of Communism.

The investor group Doug formed was able to offer the critical 400 acres at the base and helped Darcy Brown obtain options on other parcels. The Cassal ranch had been purchased by a group headed by Lew Cooley, so this large piece could be included. Darcy put together a deal for Jack and Elsie Wilson which allowed them to pay off their debt to Mrs. Wagner, receive a sizable payment, and stay on ten acres of their place rent-free for the rest of their lives in a house Jack would build starting with a $20,000 contribution from Aspen. Darcy also made a deal to purchase the house and land from Ellis and Martha Peters which gave them cash and the right to continue living rent-free in their house for the rest of their lives.

Aspen Opponents

When Aspen's actions and efforts were publicly known, the first "land rush" in the upper valley resulted. The major buyers were from Aspen, Colorado — people who had witnessed firsthand the demand for real estate near a ski resort.

At the same time the speculator group showed an interest, the "countercul-

ture" group started to move into the valley, along with a group that called themselves "urban refugees." Some members of this group were also from Aspen, but others came from California, Connecticut, and everywhere in between. Some joined the Twisp Grange, a symbol to them of rural and agricultural life. Some tried their hand at logging and a few obtained seasonal work with the Forest Service. Nearly all were well-educated, not only with college degrees, but wise in the ways to "work the system." Some were experienced in writing grants and put this skill to work. They managed to get grants for all kinds of projects from building hot houses to interviewing migrant workers.

One of these refugees was Maggie Coon, a young woman who came to the valley in 1975 to assist a former professor in preparing a planning report for the Forest Service. When the report was done, she stayed. Her mission, according to an extensive article in the *Seattle Weekly*, was to *"defeat the Aspen Skiing corporation's plans for a resort."* The article described Maggie as:

"young, college-educated, and a daughter of Eastern privilege. Only a trace of her East Coast accent remained. She is clear eyed and articulate, a natural leader of her peers."

The article goes on to explain,

"Although Maggie does, in fact, earn what money she needs to support herself, her 26-acre spread on the banks of the river was bought with money from her family, and that alone is enough to

make some of the hard-bitten ranchers fiercely resentful."

Regardless of the feeling of the old-timers, the counterculture was established in the valley in numbers. The group had strength and influenced organizations such as the Grange, and a few of the older citizens supported the group's position. It organized grant funds to support such projects as "grassroots publications" to support its cause and particularly to fight growth.

In the spring of 1975, according to the *Weekly* article, Maggie Coon decided that more cohesive opposition was needed. She made a trip to Seattle to solicit help from environmental groups. This resulted in a representative of the Wilderness Society visiting the valley and assisting Maggie, recent arrival Vicki Welch, and a few others to organize. The group called themselves the Methow Valley Citizens Council. Ironically, MVCC, as it came to be known, was also the name of an earlier organization of the community's leaders formed to promote and bring people to the

valley, the Methow Valley Chamber of Commerce.

A most acute concern of the resort opposition was the social and economic impact on the valley. Land prices in the upper valley rose as the news of Aspen's plans spread and, said Maggie Coon, prices could not be stopped from continuing to skyrocket as the development took shape. She felt that for ranchers in the northern part of the valley, the pressure for recreational homes near the resort would be enormous. In spite of the marginal and declining character of agriculture in the valley, many people felt that it was worth taking positive measures to preserve it for rural uses rather than let the land fall into overnight recreational use.

The culture of skiing was also eyed with great suspicion by those opposed to Aspen. The MVCC made much of the sport's alleged reputation for "sex and drugs." But the proponents did not equate what happened in Colorado with the plans they had for the Methow. Twisp banker and realtor Lew Cooley said that the opponents of growth did "more to upset our lifestyle than anything else possibly could."

The "anti-hippie" sentiment, justified or not, was brought to new heights as a result of the Aspen issue. A local car dealer, Abrams Chevrolet, commented in a advertisement,

"tell all of your Seattle hunters, if they don't get stampeded by deer, not to go home empty handed, take a hippie. They are kind of hard to clean, but with an apple in their mouth they make good decorations on the fenders of the car."

Mining Interests Return

Other environmental issues arose in the mid 1970s with the renewed interest in mining. This resurgence was not by the old prospectors of the gold rush days and did not involve the stock selling schemes of the first half of the 1900s. Rather, this was a sophisticated and well-funded operation. The Quintana Mining Company had claims on Flagg Mountain, located on the northeast side of Mazama facing Sandy Butte, the site of the proposed ski resort.

Quintana had not operated as openly as Aspen. It had quietly gone about the business of drilling cores to analyze the ore and stake more claims. Quintana planned to proceed with an open pit mine one mile long, one-half mile wide and 1,500 feet deep when copper reached $1 per pound, which the company estimated would be within five years. Because the ore is a low grade, the rock would be washed with massive amounts of water

and would create more severe water quality problems than any resort could possibly create. This mining issue got the attention of environmentalists and nearly everyone at Mazama.

To complicate things further, a senior citizen member of the MVCC, and a financial contributor, was a mining engineer who felt differently about mines than skiing. Questioned about why a mine would be acceptable, his response was "they're our kind of people."

So ski area proponents were now battling MVCC as developers on the one hand and Quintana as environmentalists on the other hand. They felt that the environmental damage which would be created by the mine would be drastically damaging to the resort atmosphere which attracts tourists as well as the valley as a whole. They were frustrated that MVCC appeared to take no stand on the mine, and even some of the new counterculture people felt *"mining was more in keeping with the rural nature of the valley."*

Sun Mountain and the Growth of Cross-Country Skiing

The mid 1970s saw the development of skiing at Sun Mountain. Sun Mountain had been primarily built as a summer resort and an extension of the old Sunny "M" Dude Ranch. Owner and developer Jack Baron closed the resort in the winter and hired one or two people to maintain the facilities, keep it heated, plow the road, and meet all the fixed costs, in the face of zero income. Thus, the idea of generating some rental income from groups of cross-country skiers from REI, a Seattle mountaineering and outdoor group, organized by Dave Chantler, seemed to make sense.

The first winter season was short. Jack hired Terry Haynes as a "one man show." Terry was the director of recreational activities at the resort. He played guitar, sang, and organized recreational activities. He rented some skis at the mountain, laid out trails, and did some trail grooming. However, Terry was more interested in alpine skiing than cross-country, and eventually left Sun Mountain to relocate in Aspen.

Around this time Doug Devin and his family and friends laid out and cleared x-country trails on "the Aspen property". Jack Wilson kept three of his cabins open in the winter and Doug had pamphlets printed about x-country skiing in the valley.

In 1976, Don and Sally Portman came to Sun Mountain and opened a cross-country ski shop. Don was the director of Sun Mountain skiing well into the 1990s and was instrumental in forming what would become the Methow Valley Ski Trail Association (MVSTA), the entity which laid out and groomed the trails in the upper valley. The groomed ski trails, scenic vistas, gentle terrain, and sunshine were central to the growing reputation of Methow skiing.

At first, there were many separate efforts to maintain trails with snowmobiles. Portman had the most extensive grooming system at Sun Mountain, and Jack Wilson was grooming in Mazama on trails of the "Aspen Property." Trails were started at Rendezvous Mountain and eventually developed into an extensive hut-to-hut ski experience. Dick Hamel, a Winthrop motel operator, developed trails around the town. In all, there were over 50 miles of trails at the time, which made the magnitude of the trail system noteworthy nationwide.

The first sanctioned cross country ski race in the Methow was sponsored by the Early Winters Ski Club with the help of the U.S. Ski Association. It attracted skiers from around the state, introducing competitors to the Methow Valley snow and local people to this competitive sport.

In 1978, a Mazama ski group held the first cross country ski race in the area called the "Early Winters Nordic Classic," to be officially sanctioned by the Ski Association. This event introduced many competitive skiers to the area for the first time. Jack Wilson was there in his cowboy boots, as was Claude Miller with a sleigh and a team of horses. Some Mazama ladies, including Bess Karro, baked goodies for the participants.

Nordic skiing continued at a slow pace in Mazama, because building a hill for alpine skiing was the focus of attention at the time.

Meanwhile, in 1974, Jerry Blann and the Aspen company had become a very visible part of the community and hired a helper for the task of completing the feasibility study and preliminary layout of the mountain. He was Tucker Barksdale, a young "local" man who had degrees in forestry and geology. He was the son of the well known University of Washington Professor of Geology, Julian Barksdale, who had spent a lifetime studying and writing about the geology of the Methow Valley.

By 1975, state-of-the-art technicians had planning for a major resort in full swing. A second feasibility study was completed for the Aspen directors. While all aspects of the resort looked promising from a business point of view, the permitting aspect looked difficult for the foreseeable future.

The top third of the mountain was in an unroaded area even though the bot-

tom portion had been logged. The unroaded land was theoretically a candidate for a wilderness area designation regardless of its other qualifications or circumstances. Hence, no action was possible for the land until completion of a study called RARE I and a later study called RARE II, and eventually the passage of the Washington Wilderness Bill in Congress.

In the meantime, the Provincial Government of British Columbia had been wooing Aspen to develop ski facilities at Blackcomb Mountain adjacent to Whistler Mountain. It was too good a deal to refuse, and the timing was right for Aspen to leave the Mazama project and move to Canada. The company estimated that it could develop in Canada and by then the wilderness issues would be solved and the project could be restarted in Mazama. The Canadian project went well, but before it was completed, the Aspen Skiing Company was purchased by Twentieth Century Fox and the Aspen people and all of their businesses were caught up in the great world of buy-out/spin-off mergers.

The Early Winters project was a relatively small item in the world of big resorts and movie stars, and thus went generally unnoticed at Fox for some time. Jerry Blann had been promoted to senior management, and when the option period on the real estate was up, he was able to convince the real estate division of Fox that it was a good investment. Fox purchased the property, but soon spun it off to Urban Aetna, a group involved in building high rise office buildings in large cities. It became evident that the owners would not likely be interested in building a ski resort in Washington State.

It was at this time that Doug Devin, together with people from the Methow and the Seattle people who had previously assembled the land Aspen had purchased, formed a company called Methow Recreation Inc. (MRI) and proceeded to apply for a Forest Service permit to build a ski area. Part of the option agreement with Aspen stated that if Aspen did not develop, it would turn over to the sellers (Devin and friends) all of the studies and engineering data that it had assembled. Aspen complied with this agreement and these studies, worth about a quarter million dollars, were the principal capital that started MRI on its way.

The directors of MRI were a cross-section of interest groups. The President and managing director was Doug Devin. The other directors were Scott Detro, a retailer from Riverside (near Omak); Walt Hampton, the general manager of Mission Ridge ski area; David Gossard, an attorney from Seattle; Claude Miller, a packer/outfitter from Winthrop; and Bob Ulrich, a pharmacist from Twisp. In 1978, using the studies and engineering that had been developed by Aspen, MRI officially submitted an application for a permit and supplied the data necessary for the Forest Service to start the process and write the required Environmental Impact Statement. It was a large task, and at this time was the most complex evaluation the Okanogan Forest had ever undertaken.

Throughout the 1970s, the Methow community was taking dramatic steps towards the acceptance of a new comprehensive plan and zoning ordinance, very radical at the time for a rural county. There were dozens of meetings on land use and the MVCC (Methow Valley Citizens Council), who opposed the ski area and growth in the Methow, took an active role in all of the meetings and public hearings. Members of the group were articulate and well prepared for the meetings, and usually garnered a supportive group in the audience.

Many of the locals and old-timers felt overwhelmed by the organization and apparent power of these "no growthers." The business community and much of the upper valley "establishment" including Jack Abrams, the former county commissioner, set up their own organization called "Citizens For Planned Growth" (CPG). They got contributions from the community and local businesses and hired an executive secretary, Edison "Pete" Arnold, a retired air force pilot and officer.

Pete had built a private air strip at Lost River and subdivided the area into hundreds of lots, many on the river, many in the woods, and many on the runway. The location offered purchasers the opportunity to fly their planes to this remote and beautiful place and park them in front of their own private cabins. Pete was a developer and was proud of it. He felt that proper development and recreation offered the only economic opportunities for the valley and wanted to stop the "no growth" newcomers from preventing existing landowners from exploiting these opportunities.

The CPG appeared to be relatively successful. The group signed up many members, collected enough money to keep the organization running through the time the zoning issues were current, and had a significant influence on the outcome. After Pete's success in getting public support in the zoning issue, he decided to run for county commissioner. Pete ran against Archie Eiffert, a local man, who had been mayor of Twisp. Pete and Archie were members of the same political party and, most likely because of Archie's long-time presence in the valley, Pete lost. In the end, however, Pete devoted his efforts to helping Archie win the seat as commissioner.

A great many of the issues put forward by the MVCC proved to be important for the valley if growth was to happen in an orderly fashion. There was no question by this time that growth was accelerating and if safeguards were not in place, it could become a developmental disaster. Members of the MVCC did not all share the same objectives, however. Some members were interested in planning and directing, some were simply obstructionists, some had environmental goals, and some had social goals to achieve.

By the end of the 1970s, because Mazama became the center of real estate speculation, controversy between special interest groups, and media attention, the area was no longer a secret hide-a-way. Major Seattle newspapers carried stories telling how Mazama and the Methow Valley were about to be destroyed, editorial writers told how a resort at Mazama would benefit the entire state, and television news people from Spokane and Se-

attle covered Mazama for features on the proposed resort and the people of the area. Schools and colleges from all over the Northwest included the Early Winters development as class projects for many different reasons and perspectives. It was studied in nearly every land-use class, in architecture classes, in public affairs courses, and seminars on community development, and was the focus of many a thesis and term paper. For better or worse, Mazama, Early Winters, and the upper Methow were smothered with attention.

By the 1970s, Bill and Vi Pederson had sold the Mazama Store. The new owners fixed the front, modified the name, and began enjoying winter business with the growing interest in cross country skiing.

Chapter 9

The 1980s - The Early Winters Era

The decade of the 1980s can be called the Early Winters era. Tourism showed some growth and real estate was selling like hot cakes in the upper valley. The anticipation of skiing at Early Winters was the economic generator. People were buying lots for vacation homes and property for subdivision. Young people were moving to the area with dreams of being part of the resort or starting a business in a prospering and beautiful environment. Seven real estate offices in Winthrop were all doing well.

New Arrivals and a Sad Departure

Dick and Sue Roberts arrived in 1980 with a dream of building a lodge for hikers and skiers. Dick was a handyman and did much of the construction on what Dick and Sue called the North Cascades Base Camp, which opened in 1981. Sue did the cooking and Dick provided amenities for the guests, such as skiing, which entailed his making tracks for skiers with his snowmobile. The Early Winters Project allowed Dick to bridge the river from his property and use its fields and trails, and build new trails for his guests and the community.

It was about this time that the various areas got together and formed the Methow Valley Ski Touring Association (MVSTA) and purchased professional grooming equipment. Both Dick Roberts and Don Portman took the lead in the association and assumed the risks of personally guaranteeing loans from the bank to make the organization functional.

Eric Sanford, one of the upbeat Mazama enthusiasts, was a recent transplant from Aspen, Colorado, who brought almost more ideas and activity than Mazama could handle. He billed himself as "Mr. Fun" and set up a business called Liberty Bell Alpine Tours. He sold river rafting trips, back packing trips, mountaineering and ski tours, and kayaking lessons. In 1980, Eric and his friends refurbished the old Stookey/Bowers/Eggelson ranch house, called it the Mazama Country Inn, and rented rooms to Eric's clients.

In 1982, Eric introduced helicopter skiing to the area and gained considerable notoriety for Mazama and the North Cascades as a winter sports destination of note. One success after another led to investment in a new, bigger, and better inn and restaurant which opened in 1984. But business and profits did not keep pace with Eric's enthusiasm and by 1987, the bank was foreclosing on Eric and his partners. One of his partners was Cal Merriman who ended up buying the inn at a bargain price in a foreclosure sale. Eric took up wind surfing in a serious way, sold his house and property to the Outward Bound Society, and left for the Columbia Gorge as quickly as he had arrived.

As good as things were, however, the decade was nonetheless stressful for the Mazama community. The United

States Congress finally passed the Washington Wilderness Bill which made the proposed ski hill at Sandy Butte available for permitting. Methow Recreation Inc. (MRI), which had applied for the permit, was active and expectations ran high with the cry, "Ski in eighty-three!"

———

In March of 1983, prominent Mazama citizen Jack Wilson died unexpectedly. Jack had worked tirelessly for the opening of the North Cascades Highway and was working for the ski development. Although Jack kept a string of horses for his guests at the Early Winters Cabins to ride, he had modified his trail construction business into a trail packing business and sold it to Claude Miller. Off in a new direction after the sale, Jack purchased a snowmobile and groomed tracks on the trails of Early Winters land for cross country skiers and his winter guests.

Even in light of all the attention focused on Early Winters and Mazama, there was still very little growth. There were even fewer registered voters in Mazama than in earlier times, and Kathy Grimmett, the owner of the store and post office, had to find work out of the valley to subsidize her store business and keep it open. Mazama was still in limbo.

Brian McCauley, from an old valley family, grew up near Wenatchee and was excited about the resort potential of the valley. He was a member of Governor Spellman's staff and had many contacts in government and industry. To facilitate MRI, McCauley arranged a meeting in

1984 which ended in a merger between MRI and a partnership formed by Harry Hosey of Hosey Engineering. Financing and permitting were the specialty of the Hosey firm and these elements were needed by the Early Winters project and MRI.

Enter Harry Hosey

At this time the Hosey/MRI partnership took over the project, but the applicant for the permits continued to be MRI, which was now a wholly-owned subsidiary of the partnership. Hosey had enjoyed recent success with permitting hydroelectric power projects and was enthused about the prospects of the development business Early Winters offered.

The project was funded by both the engineering company and by the family and relations of Harry's wife, Gege. Several hundred thousand dollars were invested up front to hire consultants and attorneys, and an additional million was borrowed from the Brennan family (relations of Harry's wife) as a partial payment to the Aspen Ski Company for the land purchase. Aspen, although no longer interested in development, had exercised its option and purchased the 1,200 acres at Early Winters and now wanted to sell. The fact the company wanted to sell made negotiations easier, but a considerable cash down payment was nonetheless still required.

The Early Winters Project

The logo of the Early Winters Resort.

The new management at Early Winters hired the same planning firm, Design Workshops Inc., that Aspen had retained to lay out the proposed resort. They spent thousands of dollars to update and expand the soil and hydrology studies, wildlife assessments, and other environmental studies.

With the passage of the Washington Wilderness Bill in 1984, the Forest Service issued the Final Environmental Impact Statement (FEIS) and Record of Decision to issue the permit for the ski hill on Sandy Butte. This was appealed by the MVCC group in Twisp on the last day of the appeal period, which in turn led to additional controversy between the Forest Service and David Bricklin, attorney for MVCC, regarding the timeliness of the appeal. (The Forest Service initially dismissed the appeal claiming it was postmarked late, but Bricklin charged foul play within the agency and argued that the appeal was timely, and prevailed.)

Before a decision on the appeal was announced by the Chief of the Forest Service, the proponent, MRI, entered into an extensive settlement agreement with members of the MVCC and their attorney, Bricklin, in Seattle. The Early Winters project manager at this time was Steve Excell, a lawyer by education and former member of Governor Spellman's staff. Hours of negotiations and pages of agreements covering the social and environmental concerns of MVCC were compiled. The fact that at least two, and sometimes three, of the members of the negotiating team were lawyers complicated and prolonged the process.

After several months, the negotiations reached what was felt to be a settlement which put in place guarantees of environmental safeguards, growth limitations, and funds for community and environmental purposes. At the signing meeting, however, the MVCC rejected the settlement in spite of the apparent concessions it had obtained. It appeared that any individual had a veto power of the entire MVCC, regardless of what had been negotiated. By now the MVCC had joined forces with Seattle environmental groups, most of whom knew little or nothing about the facts of the controversy, but opposed it more as a symbol of opposition to development.

Mazama Neighbors

During this same time, another group of citizens in the valley had formed an organization called "Mazama Neighbors for the Early Winters Ski Hill." While the group was founded by Mazama area land owners, its members and contributors were valley and statewide. Directors of the group included Ron Perrow, the local newspaper editor and publisher; John Rabel, a Seattle businessman, former legislator, and Mazama landowner; and Blair Howe, an Edelweiss home owner. Blair worked nearly full time at managing the group's fund raising and promotion affairs. The group claimed 2,000 members state wide at its peak of activity. The president of the group was Aaron Burkhart, a local rancher who would, ironically, be used later by opponents to bring appeals to delay the project. Graydon Patterson, son of a Mazama homesteader, served as vice president. The intent was to make the group genuinely local and grassroots.

Blair and other members and directors of the group met with opposition groups in an effort to find an area of common ground and let the media and general public know of the grass roots support for the resort and ski hill. They ran advertisements in the paper, distributed bumper stickers, issued press releases and held public meetings.

Bumper sticker.

When the MVCC declined to sign the negotiated agreement, which Mazama Neighbors felt would be good for the community, the group held a large community meeting in the Winthrop barn to explain what was happening and to enlist community support to encourage the MVCC to reconsider. Things didn't go as planned, and the meeting resulted in an

anti-MVCC surge and campaign that did little to change any opinions. Almost overnight, dozens of "MVCC buster" signs appeared in cars, homes, and businesses in Winthrop and Twisp.

MVCC buster sign.

Although the Early Winter project and management had nothing to do with the sign campaign, the negotiation atmosphere had vanished.

The Forest Service chief had been holding a decision on the MVCC appeal in abeyance, hoping that the developers and MVCC would be successful in their negotiations and eliminate the need for his issuing a decision. Obviously this didn't happen. Thus, in 1986 the Chief of the Forest Service rejected MVCC's appeal and issued a permit to MRI for skiing at Early Winters. The decision, however, included a list of requirements aimed at mitigating the concerns of the appellants. These requirements covered nearly all the concerns that had been discussed in the negotiations, from air quality to wildlife habitat to employee housing. It also included a requirement that the developers reimburse the county for any costs and that an on-going tax and assessment on the resort be established to benefit both the county and local community.

While this gave MRI a special use permit for skiing, the group did not yet have the dozens of permits necessary to build a resort or ski hill, and the permit application for the actual construction had yet to be completed. From 1985 on, permitting was in full swing. Permits were required at the state, local, and federal levels. Each agency process and permit application was a major undertaking.

From the mid 1970s, project proponents worked to see that a proper zoning ordinance was in place. This issue was generally complete, but within the county, many sub-ordinances had to be in place to comply with either the commitments made or requirements of the State or the Forest Service. To protect the perceived threat to the deer, a dog control ordinance needed to be enacted. To safeguard possible pollution from other off-site development, an elaborate water quality monitoring system was installed. To prevent air pollution, very sophisticated monitoring procedures were implemented, and the most restrictive wood burning ordinance in the state was adopted.

Every issue and every ordinance was an expensive and time-consuming experience involving public participation. In addition to paying its own staff, the project was paying the county for all time and costs incurred. An example of the frustrations experienced by both the developer and the county was the air ordinance adopted by the county after the eighteenth version had been written. Each draft was discussed with the MVCC and that group was given the opportunity to provide input. All of the group's requests were included

in the eighteenth version of the ordinance. However, during the final public hearing, the MVCC air quality spokesperson testified against the ordinance she herself had helped to draft.

The tax and assessment plan proposed would have provided considerable revenue for the county which logically created general support for the project from county and city governments. At this time nearly every elected official or government entity in north central Washington supported the project.

Public support, however, did not daunt the ski area opposition which by now was located in Seattle and included the Sierra Club and the Washington Environmental Council. These groups brought suit against the Forest Service and started a series of appeals which continued until the United States Supreme Court ruled on May 1, 1989, in favor of the Forest Service. However, two issues were not resolved by the Court and required additional permit work, thus allowing the appellants to begin the whole appeal process again.

The appeals through the federal court system were quite time consuming and expensive for Early Winters. Although the appeal was against the Forest Service, the government had minimal resources to carry the case, and MRI acted as an intervening party, picking up a big portion of the legal work and costs. It was estimated that the cost to MRI was nearly $400,000.

The MVCC and Sierra Club attorney was David Bricklin, an environmental activist expert. In spite of the fact that the Supreme Court ruled in favor of the Forest Service on nearly every issue, the Court

The developers' view of the first phase of the resort was portrayed in this winter scene of the golf course, the village, and ski hill, drawn by artist Ron Bomba, a part-time resident of Mazama.

left two issues unresolved. This, claimed Bricklin, allowed him to recover his attorneys fees from the Forest Service under the "Equal Access To Justice Act," or EAJA. EAJA is a federal statute intended to aid small business in recovering legal costs if they prevailed in a suit against a government agency. Environmental groups have successfully used EAJA to recover money when they sued the government on environmental issues. Bricklin contended that the two issues unresolved by the court constituted a victory for him and that he was owed over $200,000 in legal fees. The courts agreed and Bricklin collected from the Forest Service pursuant to EAJA.

Two other incidents occurred at the end of the 1980s that would assist the opponents of the Early Winters Resort in

achieving their goals. One was the creation of an organization called Friends of the Methow, or FOM, a Puget Sound group of environmentalists, including Maggie Coon, who owned property in the Methow or who had an interest in the area. It also included activist representatives from the major environmental groups such as the Sierra Club, Audubon Society, and Trust for Public Lands.

The other event was the attention focused on the spotted owl and the designation of the Sandy Butte area as a possible owl habitat. Considerable controversy arose over the existence and validity of any scientific evidence to substantiate the claim, but the classification stopped all development activities until the issue could be resolved. The spotted owl issue affected forests and the timber industry throughout the northwest, and carried with it consequences that reached far beyond skiing at Early Winters. Thus no decisions or appeals were considered at this time. Rightly or wrongly, downhill skiing for the present was not happening at Early Winters.

Other forces that affected the resort situation and public perception were its size and image. By the end of the 1980s the project had spent several million dollars on planning, attorneys, engineers, and consultants. In addition, the design of the project and the promised mitigation of the many environmental safeguards and contributions to social programs in the community added tremendous costs to the project. To cover these costs, the project was made larger and larger as more demands were made. When the final plans were made and published, the press reported that the resort would contain four thousand units and could have as many as 12,000 guests at build-out. This was a shock to many in the community and while it was an exaggerated, worst-case scenario, it was not at all what most people had in mind.

At this time, Harry Hosey made the decision that the project needed to control a number of adjacent acres of Forest Service land for the benefit of the resort and he proposed a land trade. Because of the urgency Harry perceived, he sought to bypass the local administrative process by getting direct legislative approval from Congress. The trade included the Early Winters campground directly on Highway 20. Although very small and not particularly pretty, it was a campground nonethe-

When the Seattle environmental groups entered the fight, they raised the level of controversy and combat with their considerable resources at hand. The Seattle opponents' vision of what the resort would look like was circulated in a flyer put out by "Friends of the Methow" showing bulldozers denuding the land.

less and therefore a "sacred cow" and an emotional issue. The opponents made good use of this issue and made conditions very difficult and expensive to get approval for the trade. While Harry succeeded in getting a bill passed which authorized the trade, the number of conditions attached made it highly unlikely that the trade would happen.

Problems in Bellevue

By the late 1980s, Harry Hosey had increased the number of partners in the Early Winters Resort Partnership considerably. Harry was a world-class salesman. He radiated enthusiasm and was never without an answer. Harry had taken over the role of project manager, general partner, and president, and raised a couple of million dollars from Puget Sound area people and a group from Chicago.

Shortly before this, Harry hired Judith Shulman, an attorney with a large Seattle firm. Judith was smart, aggressive, and had many contacts who had funds to invest. Together with Harry, they were a great team. She had the contacts, Harry had the product and the sales pitch. She gave the presentation credibility because of her legal background and because she would correct Harry when he exaggerated or wandered too far from the facts.

It was mainly Judith's contacts who were the new investors. Most of the significant investors and players in the

late 1980s were on the Board of Directors of the general partner corporation, Early Winters Resort, Inc. Harry's in-laws which included the Brennan family, were represented by Harry's brother-in-law, George Chevigny. It was through a friend of George's that Harry recruited the Chicago investors.

Judith Shulman recruited several clients, most of whom were involved in real estate as either modest developers or investors, who put in about $1,000,000. Two of them were on the Board of Directors. Doug Devin was also a director and represented the former MRI and the Mazama investors group. Doug provided the continuity from the previous studies and knew the technical aspects of the project and site. Judith acted as secretary and counsel.

Another director was Mary Ferguson. An accountant with a large accounting firm, Mary had been made

Early Winters management people stand atop Goat Wall during a planning trip to the resort site. Harry Hosey is on the right.

president of the R.D. Merrill Co., an old timber family firm with large assets in timber, real estate, cash, and securities. She was charged with managing the firm's funds. It appeared that Mary admired Judith's abilities and aggressive approach and was receptive to the presentation she and Harry made on Early Winters.

Shareholders of R.D. Merrill Co. consisted of many young third- and fourth-generation family members. Mary felt that these young people had very little interest in hearing statistics on board feet of lumber at shareholder meetings. Early Winters was an exciting project which would likely interest every one of the young shareholders. It was real estate oriented, secured, and required no active management. Harry appeared to have everything under control and she apparently thought it was only a formality to complete the permitting. R.D. Merrill Co. invested $300,000 in the project and guaranteed a loan to the project for $4 million secured by the property. Mary was added as a non-voting member of the Board of Directors.

In the boardroom in Bellevue, Washington, everything was great. Harry had hired Norb Valley to be project manager. Norb was an accountant by trade and had been a financial officer for the firm developing Wikaloa in Hawaii. Harry moved him to Seattle from southern California, bought him a new car, and started him at twice the salary of any previous manager or employee. Norb was a nice fellow, but had been so "rushed" by Harry that he evidently didn't take notice that he might not be the man for the job. After six months, Harry also realized the mistake

and paid to move Norb back to Texas where he had wanted to go in the first place. Harry admitted he made a mistake, something he rarely did, and made himself project manager. He worked harder than ever attempting to manage every little detail.

With all the new money available, Harry was spending at record rates – charter flights to the valley for any reason, dinners for local citizens, a directors' trip to Florida to see a Disney hotel, and a move to brand new spacious office quarters large enough to triple the staff. The office was complete with custom made furniture and a conference table built by Harry's brother, an iron sculptor, which cost thousands of dollars. Consultants from every imaginable discipline were hired and given instructions by Harry on what to do. Staff people assigned to work with the consultants, however, were finding their jobs difficult to manage because they claimed that Harry continually meddled in the work, changing instructions and directions.

Harry was going at a frenzied pace and doing almost everything himself. A public relations firm was hired to write a newsletter, but Harry insisted on either writing it himself or rewriting what the professionals wrote. Although the best consultants were hired, if they didn't say what Harry wanted to hear, they were phased out. The attorneys, the PR firm, and the planner were all replaced. It appeared that the worse things became, the more Harry felt he had to run everything and the more obsessed he became with control. Carol Webster, an experienced staff member who was to coordinate consultants was frequently blamed, and when she disagreed with Harry she became a prime scapegoat. Finally the situation became so disagreeable, she left.

The idea of a "heart to heart" talk with Harry about his shortcomings in management style was discussed among the directors. Hints and suggestions came up at monthly meetings, but were lost in the flurry of Harry's activity and enthusiasm. An all-day meeting to discuss the problems was planned at Semiahmoo Resort in Blaine, away from the phones and distractions, with the added benefit of seeing the facilities of Washington's newest resort. There was, however, concern over the attendance of the new director, Mary Ferguson, from R.D. Merrill, for fear of "airing our dirty laundry" in front of this new investor who was to guarantee a $4 million loan. The consensus was that Harry could be corrected if the directors could just get him to listen, and it would not be proper to show dissension or reflect poorly on Harry in front of Mary. Because of the concern over how to deal with Mary and the fact that Harry sensed that the directors might have things to say that he didn't want to hear, the meeting was canceled. Lack of resolve on the part of the directors made it easy for Harry to just forget about it and schedule other activities.

By the end of the 1980s, Judith Shulman had quit the practice of law, set herself up as a consultant at a consultant's hourly rates, and worked nearly full time for Harry and the project. She traveled everywhere with Harry and spent weeks in Washington, D.C., with him working on land trade legislation. Harry's marriage was now on the rocks and an alleged affair between Judith and Harry seemed to be the last straw for his wife, Gege, and the family.

While all this was going on, Hosey Engineering Company was falling apart, partly because Harry had been its best and main salesman and he was no longer there, and partly because Harry continued to try to manage it from afar. The employees who remained gave Harry an ultimatum — either sell the company to someone who can run it or they would all leave. A deal was finally made to sell the company to Harza, a large firm from Chicago that wanted to expand to the Seattle area. Harry had invested the company's funds in Early Winters from the beginning. In fact, those were the funds that got the project off the ground in 1985. For this, his company had been issued ownership in the Early Winters project. Neither the new owner, Harza, nor the old employees wanted this asset. Harry did, and so he received it as partial settlement for his ownership in the engineering company.

On the brighter side, by the end of 1989 and the beginning of 1990, in spite of the management problems, Harry, the staff, and the consultants had put together an impressive resort plan. The project would unquestionably be the most elaborate and complete resort in the region and, in fact, in the entire state. Considerable market research had been completed, and, at the time, the resort as planned was in great demand. Phase one of the project would likely have been very successful from a sales point of view. Everything from ski lifts to golf course irrigation was state-of-the-art. There was nothing else like it in the state and, had the plans come to fruition, the project would most likely have been a success.

If revenues met projections made by state agencies, both the county and the state would be prospering from the increased tax base and increased economic activity by the end of the second year of the resort's operation. By the end of the third year, both the state and county would be receiving a surplus over costs of services from the business and state excise taxes collected.

In addition to this revenue, the U.S. Forest Service permit that was issued

required a payback of two percent of ski lift revenues to the local community in a program to be administered by the county. This was to fund local public transportation and anything else the community felt was important. Many felt that for both government and developers, the resort was a win-win deal. However, two big "ifs" remained: permitting to allow the project and funds to make it happen.

In 1990, Jerry Blann appeared on the scene again with another attempt to bring investment money and management to the project. Jerry had left Aspen and was running a resort in California. He and an associate, Ron Miller, had made an effort to buy the ski area in Breckinridge, Colorado, but were out-bid by a Japanese

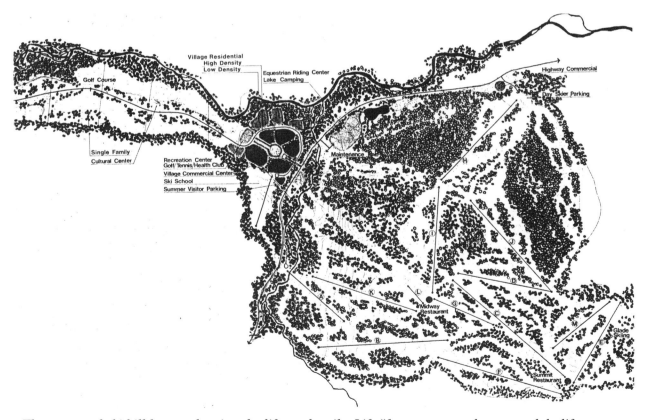

The proposed ski hill layout showing the lifts and trails. Lift #1 was proposed as a gondola lift.

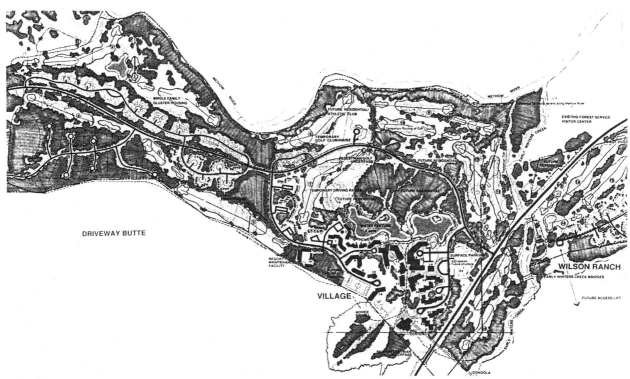

Early Winters Resort center plan proposed in 1990 designated part of the golf course on the Wilson Ranch area and on the present Early Winters campground.

group. They remained interested in getting into the ski business. Ron had been president and CEO of Disney and retained the dreams of his father-in-law, Walt Disney, to create a picturesque mountain resort village. The Disney Company had tried to develop the Mineral King area in California but had been stopped by environmental groups who opposed the project. Ron was impressed with the Early Winters project, and his site visit was the start of a series of meetings aimed at Ron becoming involved and Jerry stepping into the role of project manager. Jerry had the expertise in the ski industry and knew the details of Early Winters, having lived on site for two years and having done much of the preliminary development work on the mountain. All of

the directors felt this was an ideal solution to many of the project's problems.

The objective was to make Jerry CEO of the project and have Harry work in other areas in which he was better suited. When this became clear to Harry, he scuttled the negotiations. This was the beginning of Harry's war with the directors which eventually resulted in the removal of three of the four directors. It was said that any paranoia condition Harry might have had justifiably peaked at about this time. Staff, consultants, and even government agency people working with the project were aware of the management problems and Harry's shortcomings. County people were angry over some of his activities and the Forest Service people rolled their eyes in polite disbelief and irritation.

By this time it also became obvious to Harry's estranged wife, Gege, that she should have considerable concern for her family's investment. Her fears were confirmed by her brother, George, who was on the board and saw things even more clearly than Gege.

Harry had invested not only his wife's inheritance, but also their community property. This all resulted in a messy divorce and a struggle for control of the project management which took much of Harry's time and efforts into the early 1990s. It seemed that Harry had an obsessive need to control the project, and that this was what caused the divorce to be so difficult. Family members reported that he charmed, threatened, and pleaded with his wife, and in the end apparently the constant harassment paid off. On the advice of her lawyer, Gege gave in. Harry won the right to vote the shares of the community property. With his new control, Harry removed his brother-in-law, Devin, and another director from the board. He didn't like what Devin told him about his credibility in the community, that the project was too big for the public to accept, that his management style wasn't working, and probably most of all, that he and the other director had supported the idea that Gege should have the right to vote her share of the community property ownership shares.

The resort design concept included a compact village core with commercial outlets on the first floor and residential units above. Construction was to be with logs and natural materials and architectural styles similar to those of traditional National Park buildings.

Chapter 10

The 1990s - A New Community Emerges And the Economy Thrives

By the 1990s, there was no question that recreation and tourism were the main industries in Mazama and the upper Methow Valley. The Methow Valley Ski Touring Association (MVSTA) was grooming ski trails for cross country skiers throughout the Early Winters property and Mazama with connecting trails that went to Winthrop and the Rendezvous area to the Chewuck. The Mazama Country Inn provided fine quality accommodations and good meals for the skiers.

Cal Merriman, who had purchased HES 114, was operating the Inn and had developed a large arena and horse riding facility. There was calf roping through the summer, with special instructors brought in to teach roping. Merriman and other investors planned a major subdivision for the remainder of HES 114.

Although it appeared to be a lazy, agricultural community

because there were few houses built, in reality the area had been subdivided through the years into many subdivisions, with more than 900 lots above the Weeman Bridge. In the late 1980s, the community of Mazama had feared uncontrolled growth even with the existing county zoning ordinance, and produced a master plan for development of the commercial area. There was a consensus that too much area was designated commercial, which would lead to a sprawled town oriented towards the highway. The majority of the community expressed a desire for a compact pedestrian-oriented town off the main state highway. The county adopted the master plan, and, although most wanted a smaller commercial area,

Goat Peak rises above the Mazama Store and gas pumps in 1996. The new version of the store has a deli and lunch counter as well as an espresso machine. But, note on the extreme left of the picture that the same old gasoline pump still stands along side the modern pumps. It is, however, only for memories of past eras, as it no longer pumps gas.

most citizens felt it was better than having no plan at all.

The establishment of the MVSTA trail system gained momentum in the 1990s, and the name of the trail and organization was changed from "Ski" Trail to "Sports" Trail. The community began to see the value of the trail system, particularly to the tourism business. Helicopter skiing out of Mazama had been introduced in the 1980s and, together with skiing on machine-groomed trails, gave Mazama a national reputation as one of the country's preeminent winter sports destinations.

The momentum for the trail development came principally from John Hayes who, like many, moved to the valley from Aspen, Colorado, when the Aspen Skiing Company was proposing an alpine ski development in the area. John stayed in the valley and became involved in community activities, including the dream of the creation of a public trail from Winthrop to Lost River, with miles of side loops for skiing, hiking, bicycling, and horseback riding. Because of the miles of private property that would have to be included in the trail system, few thought it could be made to work. John Hayes, however, was a dreamer and a whirlwind of activity and energy who never tired of working towards making the system a reality.

John had been involved in a number of business deals in Aspen. He was a veteran of the Vietnam War and had been disabled while serving in the Marine Corps. He had been wounded during the war by three gun shots and an exploding grenade. He lost his left eye and wore an eye patch, but never lost any enthusiasm for life.

After his first visit and stay in the Methow in 1974, John and his wife, Rayma, spent several years traveling around the world, sailing, and working at various jobs. Rayma went to school in Texas. They returned to the valley in 1983 and started the Little Star Montessori school for children in Winthrop. Rayma ran the school and John got involved in assisting people in land development. John had a penchant for being in the middle of every happening in the community. He wanted to help, he wanted to run it, he wanted to be the authority, and he wanted to influence, all of which resulted in hours of conversations and discussions. He made great contributions to the community, donated hours of service to various causes, and would take on projects and activities regardless of whether he had the time or the resources to do so. John attained a high profile in the community and has been the driving force behind many projects in the valley.

Early Winters, 1990s

By 1991, it was clear to most that Harry Hosey was not going to be able to continue with the Early Winters project. This was a "good news, bad news" situation for many involved in the project. Many thought that with the removal of Harry, new and experienced management could be brought to the project. The bad news was that probably all or most of the investors would lose the money and time they had invested. There was also a fear, both in and out of the community, that in such a situation the property would be divided up and sold off as quickly as possible. This would result, it was feared, in dozens of small developers and speculators chopping the land into the maximum number of parcels with virtually no plan, all to the detriment of the community. Most agreed, including most of the responsible Seattle environmental groups, that such action would be a tragedy.

John Hayes had been working with members of some Seattle environmental groups and had been honored for his work in the development of the trails. With his contacts from these activities, he brought representatives of groups to meet with Doug Devin, with the idea that Devin could help direct or influence the future owners of the land. Various alternatives and strategies were discussed in many meetings, ranging from establishing a trust, to developing the project into a scaled-down version, to purchasing the land to be put in a conservancy. After the successful negotiations and sale of the 800-acre Big Valley Ranch to the Department of Wildlife, Hayes and others, such as people from the Trust for Public Lands, were optimistic that something could be put together for the Early Winters property.

The year 1992 was ushered in by R.D. Merrill making another interest payment on the note it was guaranteeing for Early Winters and starting foreclosure proceedings. As yet, the foreclosure proceedings were not publicly known, but

some people were suspect. Many creditors had not been paid and the project owed the county $30,000 for its part of a preliminary sewer study.

It was at this time that the issue of the spotted owl again came to the surface. The mountain had been considered as possible owl habitat which could put it off-limits for most development, but no owls had been found for several years and evidence that any spotted owls had ever been found was questionable at best.

The Forest Service proposed that the Sandy Butte area, a questionable habitat area, be traded for another area where owls had actually been found. This area was not classified and was slated for logging. This proposal took Seattle area environmental groups somewhat by surprise and they reacted quickly with arguments why this would not work. They enlisted the help of the Sierra Club Legal Defense Fund and hinted at legal action if this proposal were pursued. Their position was that not only was the idea of trading unacceptable, but also that the non-classified area must be promptly included in the habitat areas.

Fearful of criticism from the environmental community, the Forest Service abandoned the idea of a trade. The Sandy Butte area was declared a possible HCA (habit conservation area) on the basis of evidence that was less than compelling. In December, 1991, the *Methow Valley News* reported owl sightings in detail. The article included the following:

"teams of temporary Forest Service staff, often college students, were trained in a 24-hour long 'North-

ern Spotted Owl Inventory & Monitoring' workshop."

The following verbatim transcript of the field notes, reported in a 24-hour clock, made by the study team in 1988 was used to establish the presence of a pair of spotted owls on Sandy Butte.

• *May 27, 1988: 2050 - saw owl (fly over heads) not a GHO [Great Horned Owl], pygmy or screech. Prob barred or spotted.*

• *June 28, 1988: 2119 hrs - owl visual - no call -medium size*

• *2301 hrs - unknown owl presumed a spotted -1ˢᵗ 3 notes good - far away*

More trips were made on July 18, July 19, and August 3, with no visual sightings except: *"sighted bird fly across road and then back."*

Many feel that according to these field notes, it is questionable whether the criteria were met to designate the area a spotted owl habitat. The Forest Service said in 1991, "since 1988 additional survey work has not produced any evidence of the existence of northern spotted owls on Sandy Butte."

The Forest Service did, however, feel that although clear-cut logging was not good for the owl, skiing probably did not pose a threat, even if owls were present.

The entire owl issue was quite emotional, very political, and governed by rules that seemed to change weekly. The Forest Service pleaded for time to work out the dilemma, but Harry viewed the issue as a deal buster. Harry had been unsuccessful in raising funds and the owl was a convenient scapegoat.

According to Harry, he was unable to raise money because the "owl put a cloud over the project." The Forest Service, and most of the partners who were informed, regarded the owl as just another issue to be solved like the water, sewer, or air quality issues, but it appeared Harry used it to rationalize his failure to raise

Carving turns in the spring snow on Sandy Butte, with views of Mt.Gardner, were indefinitely postponed due to controversy and the spotted owl.

funds. The press carried Harry's story in local and Seattle papers. This irritated the Forest Service and most of the partners because such publicity was potentially damaging to the project and adversely affected the value of the real estate.

In retrospect, Harry was probably right. The owl was a "deal buster." The owl issue was never resolved. The Forest Service, after losing so many "battles" with the environmental groups, apparently did not have the stomach to continue the fight. Close examination of the alleged evidence or sightings of owls on Sandy Butte would not likely stand up to much scrutiny and would end up being an embarrassment to the Forest Service. The fact that Harry ran out of money and stopped examining the issue was probably a relief to the Forest Service biologists who would have to justify claiming that the area met the requirements for classification as a conservation area.

By the end of January, 1992, R.D. Merrill decided to get involved once it realized that the company was headed for ownership of the project through a foreclosure. Notice of the foreclosure was to be made public on February 3, and the company faced the dilemma of taking such action and having it adversely affect the project or delaying the action and allowing Harry to continue to get in a deeper mess.

On August 7, 1992, all of the assets of the Early Winters project were sold to the highest bidder in a foreclosure sale on the Okanogan County Courthouse steps, just as the legal announcement had stated.

(Actually, the sale was moved to the basement because of the wind that was blowing.) Several members of the press attended the sale, along with several MVCC activists and a handful of persons who claimed to be interested in bidding on the assets. No other bids were made, however, other than the $800,000 bid from the Merrill representative.

The Merrill Company had guaranteed a $4 million loan and had been making the interest payments of about $10,000 per month for several months. The other shareholders, along with Merrill who had made several last gasp loans to Hosey in an attempt to keep the project alive, stopped advancing any more funds. Merrill thus had about $4.5 million plus $300,000 in equity in the project and, after foreclosure, all it had was the land and a Piston Bully Snow Groomer. The rest of the partners were washed out completely losing several million dollars, and a number of suppliers and some employees were left unpaid, in the aggregate sum of about $400,000.

Enter the Lowe Development Company

At about the same time Early Winters was trying to get permits, the proposed Point Defiance Resort near Sequim, Washington, on the Olympic Peninsula was also in trouble. The resort was being financed by Mitsubishi, a large Japanese firm, and economic conditions were causing the firm to reassess its overseas investments. World economic conditions were affecting the company's operations and the expense of the delays was more than the company wanted to live with, so it pulled out. Lowe Development Company from California was doing the work for Mitsubishi and Andy Norris was in charge of the project. Lowe had been operating in the Pacific Northwest for twenty years and had done market research in the area. The company's conclusion was that the Washington State area was under-supplied with resorts.

The Hillis law firm was also working on the Sequim project, and although they were no longer working for Early Winters, members of the firm kept abreast of the situation. Doug Devin occasionally met with members of the firm on a friendship basis. Glenn Amster, who had been the partner most familiar with Early Winters, set up a meeting between Doug and Andy Norris, which resulted in a preliminary meeting with the Merrill Company.

At this time, the president of the Merrill Company, Mary Ferguson, was leaving and there was not yet a replacement. Merrill board chairman, Cordy Wagner, along with Bagley Wright who influenced the company's course of events, listened to what Andy had to say. They were impressed to the point of hiring the Lowe Company to come up with a recommendation of how to proceed from that point and eventually to manage the project.

Andy had followed the project over the years and liked it. The Pacific Northwest was one of the top three national targets of the Lowe Company for resort building. Andy and others envisioned a resort similar to Black Butte in central Oregon for the Early Winters real estate.

Andy came from a ski resort background, having spent considerable time with development in Vail, Colorado, but he was concerned about the capital requirements involved in building a major ski resort given the Early Winters situation. A scaled down resort modeled after those at Black Butte or Sun River looked like a more realistic and practical goal.

At this point, the Hillis law firm was back in the picture temporarily, looking out for the interests of the Merrill Company. The company was comfortable with the Hillis firm because Bagley Wright's son, Charlie, had once been a member of the firm before leaving to pursue another career in New York. A replacement for the retiring president, Mary Ferguson, was found in a former banker, Bill Pettit.

Together with Andy, Bill started the whole process over again, from feasibility through design, with the entire environmental approval process taking years of time and hundreds of thousands of dollars. Andy was not daunted by the environmental challenges facing the project, but the banker, Bill Pettit, saw continuing problems and massive costs. In spite of Bill's views, the former planner from Vail, Colorado, Peter Patten, was hired to manage the planning for a resort.

In August, 1993, the Merrill family, including all the company shareholders, had their annual gathering in the Methow Valley to look over their new holdings. They stayed and played at Sun Mountain, toured the Early Winters site, and had a picnic in the Shafer field below Goat Wall. The weather was delightfully warm, the sky clear, and a small stream still trickled over the falls on the rock wall. It was gorgeous and impressive. Of the approximately 15 family members present, only a couple were not supportive of the idea of the company being involved with a resort in this spectacular area. This event, together with a 1994 meeting at Sun River, Oregon, with Cordy Wagner and Bagley Wright, were probably pivotal events in the decision making process.

About the same time the Lowe Company was undertaking this project, it also got involved in a large development and acquisition project at Sun River, near Bend, Oregon. This made Early Winters a part-time assignment for Andy and things moved very slowly for many months. Much of the work that had previously been done by consultants on the Early Winters project was repeated, but because the current project was not identical to the earlier one, new work was also undertaken.

One aspect of the project that was given major attention was communication with the opponents of the earlier project. Andy and Bill met with various groups of valley people from numerous locations, businesses, and social circles to get a feel for what the community wanted to have happen at Early Winters. Andy excelled in these public meetings. He said all the right things, and the community generally had a feeling that the project was in good hands.

In addition to the local people, Andy met with Ron Judd, leader of the Seattle-based Friends of Methow (FOM). Ron owned some real estate in the valley and thus had more than the typical environmentalist's view of the situation.

He was also pragmatic and a main-line politician with influence in nearly all environmental groups as well as state government. It was felt that if anyone could bring about reasoned discussion and a practical solution, it was Ron Judd.

Out of Andy's meeting with Ron came an agreement to work for the development of the project if the agreement, and the fact of its existence remained confidential, and if the developer would agree to the following five points:

- No alpine skiing.
- No land exchange.
- No Mazama sewer.
- Support for an environmental center.
- A right to buy the land if no project was built.

With this agreement, all of the company's attention was given to the environmental groups, and, as a result, communication with mainstream Methow people and previous supporters of the project came to an abrupt halt. The Merrill Company apparently felt that the confidential agreement prevented them from meeting with others. When Merrill took over the project, the company was regarded as a "white knight," but with its lack of attention to the community, the image began slipping. From a practical point of view, Merrill didn't need the community because the community was not going to actively oppose the project. The company's attention was focused on those who were interested in stopping the project or threatening Merrill with legal action.

One of the issues that seemed important to the FOM was the concept of the environmental center. To this end, Merrill and Peter Goldman (said to be an heir of the Goldman-Sachs investment firm) each put up $25,000 to explore the feasibility of the environmental center. Goldman had visited the Methow, purchased the Gunn ranch as a vacation home, and appeared to be an active supporter of the MVCC.

In Seattle, Tom Robinson was the head of the Washington Environmental Council. He was also married to Maggie Coon, archenemy of Early Winters and the ski area. But Tom was a politically astute person and appeared to be a reasonable negotiator. He was hired to do the study and work with various factions of the environmental community. Tom worked at the task for less than a year and was relatively successful, considering the difficulty of the task, but left the job and the area apparently due to domestic problems.

Meanwhile, Peter Patten was in Seattle sifting through scientific and environmental studies and grinding out a plan and an EIS that complied with the ever-changing results of the negotiations. The year of 1994 did see some actual results in the form of a submitted permit and even some dirt turned in the area of the Early Winters cabins. Lowe was not interested in the cabin project, so a group of Merrill family members financed this portion of the project.

Lowe and Merrill had not yet actually signed an agreement or formed their partnership, so Merrill was still the owner of the land and the project. Merrill was in the asset management business and the

timber business. The company had done some real estate investing and development, but nothing on the order of the Early Winters project. The company was quiet and conservative and didn't like controversy. It was obvious that there would be a number of surprises in store for the company.

One surprise and learning experience came when Merrill started the remodel of the old Early Winters cabins. The company had received some advice and suggestions from local builders about a low-profile approach to the remodel. The company, however, selected a Seattle architect who had done work for the family, received an award for his work, had designed a multi-million dollar house for Microsoft's Bill Gates, and was teaching at an eastern university. The feelings apparently were that surely such credentials would impress local rural officials and expedite permitting.

The architect met with the county planning office representative and a state shorelines official. He informed them in detail of his varied experience and of his creative environmental ideas, and brought the officials up to date on what was happening in the world outside the Methow. The officials should have been duly impressed that the architect took the time to meet with them, but instead they dug in their heels and nothing seemed to happen for months.

The county could not seem to deal with the issue in a reasonable way. Merrill's response was to turn the matter over to the company's attorney. This caused a minor, but expensive, standoff with the county attorney. The problem was apparently resolved when the county attorney decided to run for public office and, looking for friends, relented and allowed the work to proceed.

It appeared either that Merrill had no marketing plan or that it did not intend to target families, as the cabins had always done. The popular four-person cabins were converted to one-bedroom units. To some, the cozy country cabin atmosphere was replaced by an eclectic interior of uncomfortable furniture ill-suited for families or groups. When the cabins finally opened for business, occupancy rates fell to a fraction of the previous rates. It is, however, only fair to note that a big portion of the previous business at the cabins was generated because of the rates, which were about half of the rates for the remodeled cabins.

As part of the overall product mix of the completed resort, the cabins will undoubtedly fit a niche in the market, but as an opening product, the community was not overly impressed. On the next go-round with the Wilson ranch and the lodges and the inn, things were much different, and the community was impressed.

Charlie Wright and Arrowleaf

Another significant event happened in 1994, with the addition of Charlie Wright to the development team. Charlie is the son of Bagley and Ginny Wright. His mother is a direct descendent of R.D. Merrill himself. Charlie had been an attorney with the

Hillis law firm, but left the firm a few years earlier to become involved, to a great extent, in promotion of the arts and the administration of art foundations in New York. He was lured back to the Northwest to take over the family business, partially by the challenge of the development of the Early Winters land. While this was only a small part of the Merrill enterprises, it was, nonetheless, an interesting challenge.

As it turned out, Charlie was the right person for the job. With his legal background and familiarity with land use law, combined with his personal beliefs in environmental awareness, he was well equipped to jump into the negotiation process. Charlie is soft-spoken, a good listener, and has a way of letting people know that he understands what they are saying. Folks felt he would seriously address their concerns.

It was about this time that the project took the name Arrowleaf. The name comes from the name of the

Charlie Wright at the 1996 completion of the first phase of the Wilson Ranch project.

Arrowleaf Balsam Root Daisy which blooms in abundance in the Methow Valley during the spring. In fact, some say that the origin of the name, Methow, is the Indian dialect name for the daisy.

It was also about this time that there was a great need for a personality to be associated with the project. Fortunately, Charlie was there to fill that role, and he was just right for it. He was the boss and the owner, as much as anyone could be, not just a hired hand. His presence gave the project a sense of permanence and reliability and a personal touch. Although his arrival on the scene was probably by chance, the timing was perfect.

After two years of nearly nonstop meetings, the MVCC and the FOM signed a memorandum of understanding regarding the development of the Wilson ranch. Most of the members of these groups felt that the development plan for the overall project was the best development proposal that had been submitted. While the Early Winters resort proposal had asked for a maximum build-out of 4,000 units, this plan asked for only about 600. The directors of MVCC had spent a lot of time discussing many details of the project and Merrill had conceded to nearly every request made. For example:
• Merrill agreed to have no ski hill and to put restrictions on the land forever to prevent it from being used by downhill skiers.
• Merrill reduced the density from the legally allowed density of 3.5 units per acre to 0.8 units per acre.
• Mazama residents and neighboring properties would not be allowed to hook up to the sewage treatment facilities to be constructed by the developer so as to prevent or hinder development at Mazama.
• Because the name "Early Winters" was so widely known and acted as such an economic generator, the name would not be used.
• In addition to all the items in the agreement, the MVCC would be intimately involved in planning the development.
• The developer would assist in funding a full-time environmental institute which would have long-term funding for environmental projects in other parts of the valley, as well.

These, plus many other rights and privileges, were spelled out in an agreement which took months to conclude and ended in a split among the environmental groups. The original understanding was that the plan would be approved by the environmentalists in segments.

However, state law would not permit a phased EIS. It had to be done all at once. The MVCC would not accept this, but the FOM and people from Seattle, more experienced with the law and its goals, understood and accepted the situation. Thus, an agreement existed for the Wilson ranch portion, but MVCC would not sign an agreement for the remainder of the project. Nevertheless, meetings continued and the project management attempted to comply with both the details and the spirit of the agreement they had made.

Between the beginning and the end of the negotiations, new, environmentally conscious arrivals would "discover" the Methow, get involved and start all over again, getting up to speed on the issues and what had been accomplished. In the end, the MVCC president and most of the board members who had negotiated this historic understanding resigned, exhausted. However, the group was taken over by enthusiastic new people, ready to save the environment of this valley they had just discovered.

Separate from these groups is an entity called OWL (Okanogan Wilderness League). Actually, the group's membership consists mainly of two people known as "Bernie and Lucy." It appears that Bernie and Lucy spend nearly full time stopping any growth or development they can, all in the name of the vague and lofty goal of establishing instream flows as the primary water right. They have had some success in disrupting growth in the town of Twisp by suing the town over the expansion of its water system. They delayed completion of plans at the Merrill-Wilson ranch project and have cost Arrowleaf tens of thousands of dollars by appealing and contesting the development's water rights, and by appealing state agency decisions that recognized those water rights.

Not all of the delays and obstructions in the path of the developer can be credited to the environmentalists, however. Agency bureaucrats find innumerable opportunities to cause slowdowns. In such a large and visible project as the

Arrowleaf proposal, numerous agencies are involved for one reason or another. They must be informed and sign off, issue some permit, or take some action either for the EIS or for the eventual construction.

When the state issued the water permit for the Wilson ranch and Bernie and Lucy appealed it, all the agencies stopped work for the overall Arrowleaf project. Nearly all agencies claim to be overloaded with work and any reason to lighten the load is embraced and heeded. In the case of Arrowleaf, the agencies apparently regarded the appeal as an injunction and stopped work. Even the county stopped work. The stoppage caused months of delay. The head of each agency had to be contacted, the attorney general

The first phase of the Arrowleaf Resort development included building the Wilson Ranch and this fine lodge and restaurant on the edge of a small lake. The lake was made from an old gravel quarry that Jack Wilson had allowed the State to dig, with the idea that some day a lake would be built. Jack tried to build one, but it wouldn't hold water. Merrill Company lined the lake to prevent leakage, stocked it with fish, and uses it to store water for irrigation.

had to become involved, and the year was nearly over before progress resumed.

In spite of these obstacles, the plan and the EIS were completed in 1995. After the plan and the EIS were issued, the public had the opportunity to attend hearings and submit comments. The year 1996 was well underway by the time the changes were made to reflect the public's comments and the county's requests.

In July of 1996, the Arrowleaf project opened a beautiful lodge at Wilson ranch with a small dining room and twelve luxury rooms.

The idea was to show the community the quality and sensitivity the project intended to carry through the entire resort project. Even though Wilson Ranch was open, however, the rest of the project was being protested. In September of 1996, after rejecting the MVCC's appeal contesting the adequacy of the EIS, the County Commissioners approved plans for the complete Arrowleaf resort.

It was probably not a surprise that the MVCC, in the last hours of the last day, filed an appeal of the Commissioners' decision in the court of adjoining Chelan County. Among the issues raised in the appeal are that the EIS failed to cover all

Arrowleaf wins county approval

☐ *25 years after first plan, Mazama resort gets go-ahead*

by Lee Hicks

Okanogan county commissioners have approved a preliminary development plan for Arrowleaf resort, decades after the first blueprints were drawn for the site in the upper Methow Valley.

In a unanimous decision on Aug. 20, the commissioners voted to rezone 1,208 acres near Mazama to permit construction of a year-round resort that includes an 18-hole golf course, 690 dwelling units divided between lodge rooms, single family homes and condominiums, and a retail village.

"We want to express our appreciation to the county commissioners and the planning staff," said Merrill CEO Charlie Wright after hearing the decision. "They gave careful review to the plan and committed an incredible amount of time during the process."

Tuesday's decision follows last week's denial by the commissioners of an appeal by Methow Valley Citizens Council which argued that the environmental impact statement for the project was inadequate.

In approving the preliminary proposal for Arrowleaf, the commissioners stipulated a number of conditions that the development group, R. D. Merrill Co. and Lowe Development Resorts, must address as construction proceeds.

A priority concern has been maintaining air quality in the upper Valley. The preliminary development plan included a proposal for 239 wood-burning devices, with a review process to kick in after 81 devices were in operation.

After considering their options, the commissioners decided to require a performance review after only 40 wood-

An article from the August 22, 1996, Methow Valley News.

the issues and that the EIS was too long. When, if ever, these many controversial details will be resolved is not known, but at some point the story must take a break.

Even at the time this book is being completed, events are taking place that will affect the project at Early Winters. The announcement was made that Harbor Properties, a development firm from Seattle, will be replacing Lowe as the development partner at Arrowleaf. Harbor Properties is primarily owned by the Bullitt family, another old Seattle timber legacy, that has also been active in environmental movements. It would appear that their development experience and environmental sensitivity would provide a good partner for the R. D. Merrill Co.

Nevertheless, an appeal is still pending, and based on previous events, it is fair to say that the fate of the completed Arrowleaf project is not yet sealed and opening day for the resort, while more certain, could be some time off.

———————

Meanwhile, Mazama remains a bustling country crossroads. The summer of 1996 saw the opening of a new store, a remodel of the old Mazama Ranch House, expanded tourist accommodations, and many new housing starts. But in spite of all this activity, there are still many more deer than people, and people still complain about bears getting into their apple trees, that winters come early, that it's too cold and there's too much snow in the winter, that the river dries up almost every year, and that the fishing isn't what it used to be. These comments have been made for the past 100 years in Mazama, and chances are they will continue to be made for the next 100.

Index

Postcript

In the introduction of this book it states that this story is only a glimpse of the past and present Mazama. In the future, revisions, updating, corrections and inclusions of stories that didn't get included in these pages, will be warranted. Because it is the story of a community, it needs the input from the community. Pictures and stories are undoubtedly available, but the sources were unknown to this author.

Hopefully this first effort of publication will encourage persons with information and pictures to make them available for future publication. As a start this author will act as a collection point.

Doug Devin
Star Route Box 50
Winthrop, WA 98862
or
Doug Devin c/o The Shafer Museum, Winthrop, WA

Order Form

To order additional copies of:

Mazama — The First Hundred Years

please send $19.95 plus $3.00
Shipping & Handling,
Washington residents please include 8.2% sales tax. Make check or money order payable to:

Doug Devin
Star Route Box 50
Winthrop, WA 98862

If you prefer to use VISA or Mastercard, please fill in your card's number and expiration date.
Please circle appropriate card.

☐ ☐ ☐ ☐ ☐ ☐ ☐ ☐ ☐ ☐ ☐ ☐ ☐ ☐ ☐

Signature_____

exp. date_____
_____Copies @ $19.95 ea._____
$3.00 Shipping & Handling_____
Washington State residents add 8.2%_____
Total enclosed_____

Name_____
Address_____
City, State, Zip_____

Please list additional copies to be sent to other addresses on a separate sheet.